Fernando Claudín

NLB

Eurocommunism and Socialism

Translated by John Wakeham

Eurocomunismo y Socialismo was first published by
Siglo Veintiuno Editores, Madrid 1977
© Fernando Claudín
This edition first published 1978
© NLB, 1978

NLB, 7 Carlisle Street, London W.1.

ISBN 86091 002 4

Phototypeset in VIP Times by
Western Printing Services Ltd, Bristol
Printed in Great Britain by
Lowe & Brydone Printers, Thetford, Norfolk
and bound by
Kemp Hall Bindery, Oxford

Contents

Capitalist Crisis and Socialist Alternative

The Actuality of Eurocommunism

Towards the end of 1970 a new word hit the front pages of the international press and rapidly passed into political currency: Eurocommunism. Originating outside the Communist Parties to which it referred, the term originally inspired reservations in the leaderships of these parties. This was particularly true of the Spanish party. In June 1976 at the Berlin Conference of the Communist Parties of Europe, Santiago Carrillo, general secretary of the PCE, declared that it was "a most unfortunate term. There is no such thing as a Eurocommunism." On the same occasion the general secretary of the French party (PCF) avoided the word altogether, whereas the leader of the Italian party (PCI) tacitly accepted it: "It is not a term of our invention", he said, "but the fact that it has become so widely used is evidence of the depth of the need felt in the countries of Western Europe to seek and discover new answers to the problem of transforming society in the direction of socialism."[1] Indeed, as we shall see, this Berlin conference offered the most tangible proof that a Eurocommunism did exist.

Two main arguments have been advanced against the suitability of the term. Firstly, those Eastern countries in which the Communist Parties are in power are also European, yet the term "Eurocommunism" clearly does not refer to

1. Texts on the contributions at the conference, which took place between 23–24 June 1976, published by the respective parties.

them—unless as a negative. Secondly, it can be objected that Japan is an Asian country yet the positions of the important Japanese Communist Party are very similar to those of the European parties that have been called Eurocommunist.

There is some validity in both arguments. In reality the term designates an orientation that is tending to predominate in the Communist Parties of fully-developed capitalist countries which all, within their national specificities, have certain analogous problems; in this sense the use of a geographic term is inapt. But it was in Europe that the orientation was first developed both in theory and in practice. In the event, what so often happens with a new coinage occurred with Eurocommunism; the first usage has stuck.

Shortly after the Berlin conference the same general secretary of the PCE was using the term in a report to the Party's Central Committee: "No-one could deny that there was at the Berlin meeting a substantial affirmation of that tendency which some have christened 'Eurocommunism' and which we see rather as a general project which has led to the adoption of similar positions on a series of important questions by those mass parties that operate in the developed capitalist countries, whether they be European or not."[2] He included in this *tendency* the parties of Italy, France, Great Britain, Sweden and Japan. By the close of that year Carrillo's last reservations seemed to have vanished and he launched the formula of "the Eurocommunist road to power".[3]

Two features stand out in the concrete activity of the Eurocommunist parties: (1) their effort to adapt their conception of socialism and of a strategy of transition to the specific conditions of advanced capitalism; (2) the ever sharper divergence between these parties and the "Communism" of Moscow. In Eurocommunism can be discerned the beginnings of a "Western schism" within the international communist movement, that may prove a sequel to the "East-

2. Speech to the CC of the PCE meeting in Rome 28–31 July 1976. Page 32 of the PCE publication.
3. *Mundo Obrero*, 16 Dec 1976.

ern schism" of the sixties. With it that movement has entered a new and decisive phase in its *general crisis*.[4]

But Eurocommunism has attracted so much attention not just because of the interest of its theoretical and practical problematic, but above all because the present crisis of capitalism has put on the agenda a democratic socialist alternative. This, at least, is the case in the three biggest countries of Southern Europe, where a deep economic and social crisis has combined with a crisis of the dominant political system—of Christian Democracy, Gaullism and Francoism—and where the Left is close to acquiring a hegemonic majority. It is the fact that in these three countries the Communist Party is an essential (and in the Italian case a decisive) component of the Left which gives the phenomenon of Eurocommunism its actuality on a world scale.

For the third time in this century a radical transformation of society in a socialist direction appears to the peoples of Europe as an urgent necessity, posed dramatically by the new explosion of the contradictions inherent in capitalism and imperialism. The first such conjuncture arose with the great global crisis of the capitalist-imperialist system that unleashed the First World War of 1914—whose main revolutionary result was the victory of the Russian Revolution. The second great global crisis started from the world economic depression of the thirties and reached its climax in the Second World War of 1939–45. Its principal revolutionary results were the defeat of the fascist powers, the creation of favourable conditions for the subsequent victory of the Chinese revolution together with other anti-imperialist upheavals and the dismantling of the old colonial system, and the liquidation of capitalism in those East European countries bordering on the Soviet Union.

But in none of these conjunctures was the international workers' movement in a condition to move from capitalist crisis into socialism. In Russia and subsequently in the other East European countries the conditions in which the revolution

4. See F. Claudin *The Communist Movement*, London 1975 for an account of the historical origins of this "generalised crisis".

occurred did not allow for the kind of socialist development that had so long been cherished by the most advanced
sections of the proletariat and people. Neither in the former
tsarist empire nor in those countries from which the fascist
forces were expelled by Soviet armies did the destruction of
the old regime lead on to the development of a popular
workers' democracy, the appropriation and revolutionisation
by the labouring masses of the means of production, and
increased mass participation in the running of society. Instead
a contrary process was set in train, which developed industry
and culture while depriving the workers of all social, political
and cultural freedom, leading to a new social regime with
classes of rulers and the ruled.

In Central and Western Europe between the wars, the
workers' movement and the forces of democracy as a whole
suffered tragic defeats as Italy, Germany, Spain and other
countries fell under fascist or semi-fascist dictatorships. After
the Second World War the conditions created by the victory
over fascism enabled the working class movement to win
important social reforms and improvements, to defend
democracy or to launch new struggles for its reconquest (as in
Spain, Portugal and Greece), and to strengthen its class
organisations—but all these developments took place within
the framework of capitalism.

During this period the industrialised capitalist countries
experienced a spectacular economic growth and relative political stability over two decades. From 1914 to 1945, in spite of
the international impact that the movements of national liberation, especially the Chinese, were already registering, the
"storm-zone" was essentially centred in Europe. Now it
drifted out to the periphery of the imperialist system. Germany, Japan, Italy and Spain witnessed an epoch of economic
"miracles"; learned works asserted the end of capitalist crisis
and capitalism's new ability to plan and regulate itself, and
proclaimed that the working class had been irreversibly integrated into the system and Marxism was obsolete. But with
the incipient crisis of the international monetary system in
1967, followed by social and political crisis in France and Italy

in 1968–9, the rosy prospect of neo-capitalism began to be troubled by mounting storm clouds. Today few would deny that the events of the French May and the Italian "hot autumn" were not so much isolated summer storms as warnings of bigger explosions to come. They were the beginning of a new global crisis of the capitalist-imperialist system. Eurocommunism is in large part a product of this crisis; its future will depend on its performance within the crisis.

The Nature of the Crisis

The present crisis is not economic alone, but social and political, moral and ideological. In one way or another it affects not only the industrialised capitalist countries but also the Third World and the so-called socialist countries. Hence its *global* character, although it is the economic aspect that appears to loom largest in most cases at present. But in the Latin countries of Europe which are the principal setting of Eurocommunism, it is the political aspect of the crisis which is already—or is becoming—dominant.

Among the basic factors that are common to the situation of all the Western countries the first is a new *long-term structural crisis* of the capitalist economy (the fourth of its kind in capitalism's entire history), which has succeeded the *long-term expansion* which ran from 1948 (1940 in the case of the United States) until 1967. As in the previous cases, the essential content of this structural crisis lies in the exhaustion of the previous model of accumulation, of the motor force of certain industries (in this case of the automobile industry and consumer durables in general, and of the "functional" urbanisation which accompanied them), in the obsolescence of a particular form of the international division of labour and the relationship between the centre and the periphery of the system.

After the end of the Second World War (in the USA, during the War) various economic and political factors led to a spectacular and lasting increase in the rate of extraction of surplus value and consequently of the rate of profit in advanced capitalism. Mandel, for example, singles out the following determinants: the relative weakness of the workers' movement consequent on the defeats it suffered between the two world wars; the considerable expansion of the reserve army of labour (and of the proletariat as a whole) due to the massive migrations from the land that have been a feature of capitalism since the last decade of the nineteenth century and the first decade of this, and to the massive entry of women into wage-labour; the relative reduction in prices of raw materials and a decrease in the relative costs of fixed capital, which meant that in spite of progress in semi-automation the organic composition of capital rose less rapidly than might have been expected.[5] The consequent recovery in the rate of profit, which had remained depressed for a long period between the wars, gave a new impetus to the accumulation of productive capital and was an important factor in the third technological revolution; while the other major stimulus to science and technology was the military requirements of World War Two and the "local" wars and generalised rearmament that followed it. Every branch of manufacturing industry and many sectors of distribution were transformed by the forms of semi-automation of this technological revolution, which stimulated new and vigorous investment.

But the factors that produced the spectacular growth of the fifties and sixties in the end started to alter or reverse. In many countries, as full employment set in and reserves of labour started to dry up, the balance of forces in the labour market changed dramatically. The rate of exploitation was stabilised or even reversed by a new rise of workers' struggles. The long period of relatively low raw material prices had determined lower profits and therefore lower investment in that sector; the combination of this investment starvation and various political factors then gave rise to a sensational series of price rises that once more attracted investment back to the

5. Ernest Mandel, "La recession generalisée 1974–1976 de l'économie capitaliste internationale" in *Critiques de l'économie politique* 24–5, April–September 1976, Paris.

primary sector. Above all, the "pilot" sectors of the long expansionist period, yielding superprofits and monopoly rents, attracted growing quantities of additional capital, thereby finally ensuring the disappearance of superprofits and even the emergence of excess capacity in these sectors. The rates of profit of the monopoly sector and the competitive sector eventually converged or even equalised. Meanwhile, the third technological revolution was coming to a halt. New industries were no longer being created, the innovations of the previous period were merely generalised. In Mandel's view the combination of all these factors produced a tendency for the rate of profit to fall, inevitably leading to a reduced rate of capital accumulation and a long-term decline in economic growth.

The conjunctural recession of 1974–5, occurring within this framework of structural reversal,[6] unleashed the first great generalised crisis of overproduction that the capitalist system had known since 1929. Unlike its predecessor, the new crisis was the result of a decrease in investment in all the capitalist countries (itself the result of the lower average rate of profit). The anti-inflationary policies pursued by most governments in 1973 and the first half of 1974 only exacerbated the problem; the accelerating rate of inflation was not an accidental phenomenon but the necessary consequence of techniques that governments had been using over a period of years to offset the tendency of the rate of profit to fall.

If we are to understand the way in which Eurocommunist practice has developed and will continue to develop, it is essential to keep constantly in mind the long-term structural nature of the economic crisis and therefore the dominance of conjunctural recessions over recoveries within it. We should also note, however, that in spite of certain basic similarities to

6. These long waves should not be confused with the classical cycles of expansion and recession (crises of overproduction), although they have the same root: changes in the tendency of the rate of profit, whether over a short or a long term. The difference is that during a long wave of expansion, such as that between 1946 and 1967, short-term periods of expansion predominated over brief fairly mild recessions, while in the long waves of structural crisis the expansionist cycles are shorter and the periods of recession deeper and more prolonged.

previous crises of the same type, there are certain distinctive features in the dialectic of the present crisis.

In the first place, unlike the thirties, the West European working class confronts the crisis from a position of unprecedented strength. After playing a leading role in the Resistance against fascism in the Second World War, it has fortified its class organisations for twenty-five years in successful struggles for partial improvements and reforms, and on several occasions—especially in those countries of Southern Europe where the economic crisis is now combined with a political crisis—has unleashed important offensive actions. The attainment of full or nearly full employment over a long period and the linking of wages to increases in the cost of living has lent a new objective weight to the needs of the working-class and to its own consciousness of them. In the most advanced sections of the class the same is true of demands for workers' control within the workplace, which produce an even more fundamental conflict with the system.

In other words, the powerful struggles of the European proletariat (including many channelled through the most reformist organisations) increasingly impeded the normal workings of capitalism's basic mechanism, the relationship between labour and capital, even during the phase of post-war expansion. Today the past gains and present strength and consciousness of the workers' movement represent yet further obstacles to the attempts of the directing centres of capitalism to overcome or attenuate the structural crisis.

A second factor that differentiates the contemporary crisis from that of the inter-war period is the existence on the ex-colonial periphery of imperialism of a mass of peoples and states that are actively struggling for their economic independence and development. For more than a quarter of a century the USA played the card of "decolonisation", at once to weaken and subordinate European capitalism to itself, and above all to assist indigenous ruling classes to combat the revolutionary potential of national liberation movements. Although this policy was defeated in a number of cases (China, Vietnam, Cuba), in most of the Third World countries the national bourgeoisie successfully consolidated its dominion and won concessions from the former imperial power. The active intervention from the periphery of popular movements and of bourgeois classes, simultaneously dependent on and competitors of the metropolitan bourgeoisies, did not exist in the thirties. It has undermined the stability of the imperialist system's unequal exchange between periphery and centre and constitutes another important constraint on the policies that the capitalist centres can adopt to counter the crisis.

A third important factor—and one which represents an advantage for capital today as compared with the inter-war period—is the much greater degree of "organisation" of the capitalist mode of production. We should not fall into the trap, because the neo-capitalist ideology of the end of any risk of major crisis by the ability of the system to plan has proved an illusion, of assuming that it has no planning capability at all. The reality is that the considerable expansion of State capitalism, both in quantity and quality, the links between State and monopolies, the growth of the multinationals and the existence of the US superpower as a hegemonic co-ordinating centre, all permit capitalism in the seventies to intervene more effectively than in the thirties, using its techniques of inflation and deflation to take the explosive edge off contradictions, and lending aid to the weaker links which necessarily have to take more than their fair share of the burden of any crisis. By these means, the major imperialist countries have so far managed to avoid any brutal drop in production or rise in unemployment on the scale of the inter-war years.

Of course, these palliatives are not merely the result of improved techniques of intervention by the capitalist centres, but also of increased combativity by the working-class. Yet reciprocally its greater degree of "organisation" and intervention also mark capital's increased ability to deal with the rising power of labour. So far it has managed to avoid any brusque rupture in the socio-economic fabric; but who knows what the future holds? What remains intractable is the depth and long-term nature of the structural crisis. Capitalism has been unable to prevent a drop in the average rate of profit and a major rise in unemployment; unable to find any basic remedy against inflation, obliged to have recourse to the drastic therapy of "austerity policies". No sooner had the first signs of a slight upturn appeared in the second half of 1975, than the OECD predicted further decline of economic growth indicators in 1977.[7] If there is no room for a catastrophic view, the idea that the crisis can gently run its course within easily tolerable limits is equally misplaced. If palliatives can avert disastrous disorders at any particular moment, it is at the price of dilating the crisis over time.

The structural crisis of the economy has developed in the context of a more general crisis of ideology and morality, a "crisis of values" which is more difficult to measure but has a profound practical significance. Neo-capitalist ideology has taken a severe blow. The widely held illusion among wage-earners that capitalism (albeit under the spur of political and trade union action) was capable of assuring full employment and a continuing increase in purchasing power has evaporated. This crisis of confidence in the capacity of the system has now extended to the socio-economic theory and moral repute of the ruling class. The Watergate and Lockheed affairs are widely seen to be merely the symbolic tip of an immense iceberg of corruption among the retainers of the system. The smell of scandal hovers over capitalism today.

At the same time, the old idea that capitalism has an unlimited capacity to develop the forces of production—an idea imbued with nineteenth century optimism in mankind's uninterrupted lineal progress, which also undoubtedly affected Marxism—has given way to a new awareness of the destructive impact of this mode of production. It is now realized that capitalism not only exploits and subordinates the principal factor of production—man—but that in its blind barbaric greed it also drains the planet's natural resources. It is already possible to predict that if the present mode of

7. According to the report prepared for the meeting of OECD on 22–3 November 1976 in Paris.

production continues the point will come where the balance between development and destruction tips to the side of destruction, leaving mankind in an impasse. This new *ecological consciousness*, which did not exist during any previous crisis, is another element fomenting subversion and demonstrating the need for a different kind of development, of social relations, of way of life. (Naturally the capitalist mass media have sought to manipulate and recuperate it to justify reduced growth rates and austerity policies.)

Another departure from previous capitalist crises is the fact that today advanced thought, including the new creative Marxism, is well aware that science and technology, the organisation of labour and productive forces, schools and university, family and sexual morality, culture in general, are none of them neutral but assist in the reproduction of capitalist institutions and capitalist ideology and thereby share in the general crisis. If the system is to be defeated the struggle to revolutionise these areas is as essential as the revolutionary transformation of the State and cannot be separated from that central task.

There is another sense in which the present crisis is a world crisis—including the "socialist" as well as the capitalist countries. For the contraction of the capitalist markets has determined a fall in the level and the price of Soviet-bloc exports, reducing their capacity to import capital goods and resulting in lower growth rates. This effect is combined with problems inherent in their own economies—imbalance, production bottlenecks and low productivity. In ideology, morality and culture too the world of the new dominant class of state functionaries exhibits a "socialist" counterpart to the "crisis of consciousness" in capitalism. The peoples of this opaque world believe ever less in its "socialism", in its ideology so divorced from reality, in its cultural and moral values. The ubiquitous and omnipotent State machine which has deprived them of freedom for so many decades and now seeks to channel public consciousness into the most vulgar form of consumerism, may have created resignation and political cynicism among the broad masses; but periodically antagonisms and conflicts surface explosively. The warning signs of further eruptions are abundant these days.

In this world crisis, unlike its previous predecessors, there is at least for the moment little question of the outbreak of a "world war". Yet "local" wars, and through them or in other ways the dangerous chess that the two superpowers and their satellites play against each other, with its balance of nuclear terror and giddy arms race, have had their share in the genesis of the present crisis. The Maoist thesis of an *inevitable* third world war is a mere abstract fatalism; but the threat of an apocalypse on the horizon is undeniable. There is no justification for the belief that the threat of reciprocal nuclear destruction is sufficient to prevent it, nor can much faith be put in obscure double-dealing, or precarious compromises such as the Helsinki agreements. Such hopes can only lead to dangerous demobilisation, for no lasting peace is possible without the disappearance of capitalism and the dismantling of the present Russian regime. Because the crisis has widened the gap between rich and poor countries and sharpened the contradictions between the two blocs and within them, international relations are now less stable and the risk of local wars that might include the use of nuclear weapons, and even of a new world war, has increased.

As in every previous crisis, its possible resolution is not predetermined by fate—only the course of the class struggle in the major countries and the trajectory of international relations (the two being intimately connected) will decide the outcome. In theory, as Samir Amin has argued,[8] various forms of reconstruction are open to capitalism—a new motor force could be created, based on a new model of accumulation, through massive investment in nuclear or solar power, space, genetics, the production of synthetic foodstuffs, the exploration of the ocean floor, etc; or there might be new forms of state intervention, of capitalist concentration or competition, a new division of labour between the centre and periphery of the system (the most likely version would dis-

8. Samir Amin, "Une Crise Structurelle", in *La Crise de l'Imperialisme*, Paris 1975.

place the older industries—steel, chemicals, motors and light industry in general—to the periphery, while the new industries were concentrated at the centre). Another important outlet for any capitalist reconstruction might be the penetration on a grand scale of the markets of the Eastern bloc.

But all possible capitalist solutions of the present crisis would take a long period to work out and would involve enormous social tensions, contradictions and conflicts. Some elements of the above theoretical anticipations are already present in the policies of the major Western governments, but essentially their objective is the restoration in the short or medium term of the previous mechanisms without any major structural change. The only way the working class can prevent the crisis being solved at its expense is by struggle. If that struggle flags, if the left cannot reinforce its unity and win new allies, if it proves impossible to construct a socio-political bloc broad enough to develop an offensive strategy in the struggle for power and for radical reforms, capable of initiating the transition to socialism, then the forces of conservatism will be able to impose *their* "austerity policies" within the framework of more authoritarian political regimes, and so to prepare the ground for a new expansionist phase of capitalism.

This is the historical challenge that confronts Eurocommunism and all genuinely socialist forces in Europe.

Political Crisis in Italy, France and Spain

The global nature of the crisis, and especially its political dimension, can be seen most clearly in Western Europe. In the present historical conjuncture these countries may prove to be the weakest link in the imperialist system. Let us single out three central processes.

First, there is the gradual construction of a capitalist Europe sufficiently integrated economically and politically to make it a third superpower, and so potentially able to contain working class upsurges. The economic crisis and the unloading of its worst effects by the USA onto Europe have dealt a severe blow to this process. It is true that the economic basis for integration at the level of European monopolies has been broadened by the acceleration of capitalist concentration, while the European ruling classes have increased their efforts to turn the European parliament into an adequate instrument against the Left. But at the same time the crisis has led to an aggravation for a considerable period of inter-state and inter-imperialist contradictions which the workers' movement can turn to its own tactical and strategic advantage—not only at the national level, but also in the struggle for a workers' Europe.

Secondly there is the crisis of Social-Democracy. In Germany, Britain and Scandinavia, in a context of economic growth, full employment, welfare state and periodically negotiated increases in real wages, Social-Democracy has been the supreme form of political mediation between capital and labour ever since the Second World War. The most recent elections have shown that this role is now being challenged by the most conservative elements of its own social base at the same time as left currents are developing within its ranks. It is by no means certain that the working classes of Northern Europe will remain resigned to a long-term reduction of their previous economic and social gains—particularly if the possibility of Left governments within which the workers' parties hold hegemony becomes a reality in Southern Europe.

It is in Southern Europe that the third and most significant element of the European crisis is to be found—that which may make Western Europe in a very direct sense the weakest link of the imperialist system in the present world conjuncture. For in the South, there is now no mere political instability involving changes of government, but a crisis of the political regime which is tending to develop into a crisis of the social order. In less than three years we have seen the collapse of the dictatorships in Portugal, Greece and Spain, while in France and Italy the balance of forces has swung substantially towards the Left. Of course, the process of struggle between the forces seeking a way to socialism and those seeking to preserve capitalism is only beginning and has not been resolved in any of these countries; the outcome is still open and may well not be decided for some time.

In Greece, where in spite of a potentially strong social base the Left was divided, the bourgeoisie was able with the assistance of part of the military high command, to take advantage of the Cypriot adventure and jettison the colonels' dictatorship without any serious trauma, ensuring its continuity of power within a new parliamentary regime. In Portugal the wave of revolution has receded, leaving behind an advanced Constitution and most of its economic and social gains; at present there are some signs of a recovery by the Left. The Soviet orientation of the Communist parties in both countries (or at least of the larger of the two Greek parties) was an important contributory cause of these setbacks.

Subsequent developments in both countries will be greatly affected by what happens in the three crucial nations of southern Europe: Italy, France and Spain.

In *Italy* the elections of 20 June 1976 marked a spectacular advance by the Communist Party. Although Christian Democracy made a small relative gain, it has now lost its political hegemony, while the Left as a whole is henceforward close to an absolute majority. After the elections, social and political struggles radicalised over the central problem of what solution to seek to the crisis: policies aiming at a transition towards socialism or at a reconversion of capitalism? The PCI's prudent general secretary, who is not normally inclined to be overdramatic, declared in a report to the party's Central Committee in October 1976[9] that the "generalised crisis of Italian society" had reached a "breaking point", what Gramsci called "the limits of social toleration". Starting from the assumption that some kind of austerity policy was inevitable, Berlinguer argued that such a policy must be "socially equitable and—the second non-negotiable point—must serve as a policy for the transformation of society". Which, he added, requires that "it should not depend on the spontaneous laws that operate in capitalist society, nor on

9. *L'Unità*, 18 and 22 October 1976.

the mechanisms of the state machine as they now operate".

Christian Democracy and the Confindustria (the main employers' organisation) have meanwhile sought to impose an austerity policy of an opposite character; their aim is to restore those "capitalist mechanisms" to the benefit of Italian and international big capital; to strike at the standard of living of the masses and, most importantly, to attack the gains which Italian workers had won on the trade union and political fronts in the great struggles of 1967–69. These include the sliding scale (automatic pay increases to take account of increases in the cost of living), plant-level bargaining, workers' control over conditions in the factories, trade union facilities within the workplace, increased popular intervention in political structures (municipalities, regions and parliament) and in the apparatuses of repression (courts, police and army) and of ideology (education, family and information). In short, the goal of the Italian Right is to make use of the crisis not just to restore "normal working" of the capitalist mode of production, but to inflict a historic defeat on the forces of the working class and of Italian democracy.

The indecisive balance between these two alternatives, these two different "austerity policies" has been reflected in a series of uneasy governmental formulas. If the balance tips one way it will lead—as the *Manifesto* group fears—to a loss of support among the Left's social and political base and a possible return to Christian Democrat absolutism. The alternative outcome would be for part of Christian Democracy to swing to a position of open collaboration with the Left, allowing that "democratic union"—of Communists, Socialists and Christian Democrats—which the PCI so desires.

In *France* the decomposition of the reactionary government bloc has accelerated as the Left has advanced. If there is no unforeseeable political or social change, the victory of the Left in the municipal elections in March 1977 will be repeated in the general election in March 1978.

Gaullism, which had been badly shaken by the May events of 1968, began to decline with the General's death. By 1974

Giscard d'Estaing, a representative of the classic Atlanticist right, had become head of state. An important section of the Gaullist bloc led by Chirac chose to back Giscard rather than risk a victory by Mitterand as the sole candidate of the Left. However the Gaullist party, the UDR, still possessed a parliamentary majority within the government bloc and Giscard named Chirac Prime Minister as payment for services rendered. But this compromise between Giscard and Chirac—between the classic Atlanticist right and the populist nationalist right—could not stand the strains of the capitalist crisis. Underlying differences became more acute, in foreign affairs as much as internal policy. Giscard's Atlanticism became more and more subordinate to the interests of US policy and the multinationals, sharply at odds with the nationalist tradition of Gaullism which represents the interests rather of the national bourgeoisie, large sections of older intermediate layers and portions of the technocrats.

Each of those Right-wing forces sought to stem the Left's advance at the expense of the rival group. Giscard sought to isolate the Communist Party by drawing the Socialists into a reformist bloc of the centre, thereby reducing his dependence on the Gaullists. In class terms this meant an alliance between big capital, the technocrats and the most prosperous and reformist sections of the workers' movement, with the aim of solving the crisis by renovating a now outdated French capitalism. Although the workers would pay the real price, this would also damage the old middle classes and some fringes of the bourgeoisie. Chirac's plan, once he was in direct opposition to Giscard in the new Gaullist RPR (Rassemblement pour la République), was to meet the Left head on, grouping all the most traditionalist classes and layers of French capitalism together with the modern national bourgeoisie under an anti-communist, anti-socialist, anti-collectivist banner. He also hoped by the use of a certain social demagogy, appealing to nationalist sentiments and Resistance traditions, to draw in sections of workers. Although he had been a Minister in every government since 1968 and Prime Minister since 1974, Chirac now threw all responsibility for the handling of the economic crisis onto Giscard in order to present himself as a new saviour of the nation—as if he had no responsibility for the general crisis of French society.

The leaders of the Left are undoubtedly correct when they warn against any underestimation of the dangers inherent in such a Bonapartist project and against any easy assumption of victory in the 1978 elections. If the Left is to defeat both Right-wing strategies it must learn to make use of the Right's internal contradictions and win over as far as possible those sections of the working class and the population who are under the influence of Gaullist populist nationalism or of the Church. The unity of the Left, which was greatly strengthened by the presence of unitary Left candidates in most of the towns of over 30,000 inhabitants in the municipal elections, must be further reinforced. Above all the Left must develop the popular working class offensive against Giscard's capitalist austerity plan. The general strike and street demonstrations of 7 October 1976, the biggest since May 1968, and the subsequent mobilisations, have shown the way forward. If the Left continues along this road, then the 1978 general election may well have the historic significance of initiating a process resolutely oriented towards the democratic-socialist alternative.

In *Spain*, Franco's death in 20 November 1975 merely accelerated a process of decomposition of the regime which was already far advanced. A number of factors had combined dialectically to bring about the process. Spain, which in the thirties had been an agricultural country, was now a fully capitalist industrial society, a transformation which has led to increasing contradictions between the interests of the capitalist class and the Francoist state structures. The workers' movement had recovered from the great defeat of the Civil War, and acquired new features that made it qualitatively and quantitatively one of the most advanced in Europe. Growing resistance in the nationalities and regions challenged Francoist centralism. The European context of the EEC was also exerting some pressure. Finally the world economic crisis exacerbated all the tensions and contradictions specific to Francoism and its economic structures.

But although the dictator had disappeared, the forces of democracy still did not have the influence in the country nor the degree of unity or organisation needed to achieve their immediate objectives. Much of the population remained paralysed, whether by fear of repression or by political indifference or scepticism. Nevertheless it was obvious that the demand for freedom and democracy would develop very fast in the new situation. Every day more elements of the ruling class, in industry, in politics, in the army, understood that if they were to preserve the social order they must change the political order. It was equally obvious that the monarchy—the key piece in the reformist game—would only be retained if it acceded to this objective need of Spanish capitalism.

Juan Carlos understood and immediately dropped the historic function that Franco had assigned him when he declared him king-designate; instead of the supreme guarantor of Francoist continuity he became its illustrious gravedigger. Thereupon the reformist initiative of the ruling class, in dialectic with the social and political awakening of the population, produced massive struggles on the part of workers who refused to bear the costs of the crisis which the employers and the government sought to impose on them; an explosion of nationalist and regionalist aspirations; demonstrations on every kind of social or political issue; the open organisation of political parties and trade unions; a mass of critical, progressive newspapers and journals.

Another product of this dialectic was the collapse of the Arias-Fraga style of reformism, still too Francoist, in favour of the Suarez style. Suarez proved much more responsive to new popular pressures, and so managed to win over the moderate opposition and at least temporarily confine the Left within the bounds of a reform which, although it marked the end of Francoism, was still a long way from the full democracy that the working-class and popular movement had set as their immediate goal. In the present socio-political situation in Spain any further opening in the struggle for a democratic alternative can only come from a change in the balance of forces in favour of the Left and more particularly the workers' movement. Only if the main components of the Left—Socialists, Communists and the Left of the national and regionalist movements—show political sense and ability to cooperate will the democratic alternative develop along its potentially socialist road. The present dynamic makes it likely that before very long events will have moved beyond the probable result of the June elections (to be held in conditions of the most rudimentary democracy).

Thus, in spite of their different origins the socio-political processes that are in train in each of the three key countries of southern Europe, have certain essential features in common. What is at stake is not simply a change of government or of policies, but a fundamental change of direction of the society as a whole. In each of these weak links of mature capitalism the global crisis of the system poses the concrete question: is the crisis to be solved by an "austerity policy" which imposes the main burden of sacrifice on working people, while repairing the mechanisms of capitalism to equip them for a further prolonged period of existence—a solution which it would be difficult to conceive without a turn to more authoritarian policies? Or will the solution of the crisis introduce profound changes of economic and social structure which, even if they still involve sacrifices on the part of the masses, allow some sense of what a transition to socialism might be? The second option would necessarily involve the extension and deepening of democratic involvement in the political arena as well as in production, the hegemony of working class and popular organisations in the State and in civil society, and radical changes in the structures and apparatuses of the State.

Another phenomenon which marks a difference from the other advanced capitalist countries and puts the possibility of a democratic socialist alternative directly on the agenda in France and Italy (and soon in Spain too) is that the forces fighting for socialism in politics, the trade unions and in culture can already count on the support not only of the majority of workers, but of important sectors of the new intermediate layers and other social groupings. The present dynamic of the socio-political process in these three countries allows us to predict that in the short or medium term the forces of socialism will have a clear majority in a qualitative as well as a quantitative sense, numbering on their side the best qualified and most active elements in economic production and in culture.

A third feature common to all three countries is that the socio-political bloc capable of introducing a socialist transformation is axed around a combination of socialists and communists. The balance between the two elements varies in each country; in Italy it weighs towards the Communists in every respect; in France the Socialists have the advantage in the electoral arena but the Communists in the degree of organisation and implantation in the working class; in Spain too the Communists have a greater weight in the working class and we have yet to see whether, as now seems probable, the elections yield a Socialist superiority similar to that in France.

We could list many other similarities, as well as many more or less relevant differences, but for the moment let us limit ourselves to these three, plus one very important factor which affects the process in all three countries—their relative synchronisation. The global capitalist crisis has acted as orchestral conductor, bringing each separate process into play with the others. The effects of this synchronisation are already noticeable. They could become much greater, operating sometimes in a positive and sometimes in a negative sense. If the present dynamic of a Left advance continues, however, they could assist the three countries to make a combined front against common (external) enemies.

At present it is only in these three countries of Southern Europe that there seems any likelihood of a democratic alternative leading into socialism. Yet although it would only apply to a limited geographical area, the international impact of such a development does not need to be emphasised. Kissinger underlined the strategic importance of the region in a speech to the US European ambassadors in December

1975:[10] "The progress of left-wing politics (in Southern Europe) threatens to undermine the security relations and defence policies on which the [Atlantic] alliance was built. This progress is also bound to affect relations between Western Europe and the United States. We have witnessed a growth in the influence of the Communist Parties in Italy, Spain and Portugal, and possibly in France [Kissinger was speaking before the Left won a majority in the French municipal elections]—we have to ask ourselves what we should be doing about it." Since that time various US political and military leaders have made "suggestions" as to what should be done. (In the last part of this essay we shall refer to the answers that have been proposed by Carter's team of advisers.)

The international concern that a democratic socialist alternative should not take root in Southern Europe is based on the contagious effect it would certainly exercise on the other peoples of Europe (and of other continents). The impact would be most direct on countries like Greece and Portugal where, as indicated above, the present balance of forces is extremely unstable and the Left still retains an enormous potential. But it would also be felt in the classical homes of Social-Democracy, where the left currents that are on the rise in the British Labour Party and in German and Scandinavian Social-Democracy would receive a new fillip. Mitterand has correctly stressed that a Left government in Paris "would exert a tremendous ideological influence on the English and German workers". This influence would extend also to the peoples of Eastern Europe, where in spite of the repression which forces them underground, very real currents pressing for democracy have developed which look for solidarity to the Eurocommunist Parties—the vigorous movement of intellectuals and workers in Poland, the nascent Left in the USSR, the opposition which has survived the "normalization" process in Czechoslovakia. The example of a European advance towards democratic socialism would also contribute to the awakening of the US working class whose ideological and

10. *Le Monde*, 14 April 1976.

political integration into the capitalist order has been one of the firmest foundations of imperialism.

It is in this context and this perspective that the actions and historic responsibility of the three major Eurocommunist parties must be viewed; in the following chapters we shall analyse how their positions have evolved, beginning with their separation from Moscow.

2.

Eurocommunism and Moscow

The Historic Roots of the Conflict

Those who consider Eurocommunism to be no more than another tactic behind which lies the "hand of Moscow" are mistaken. Although there still remain certain contradictions and ambiguities, the major Communist Parties of the capitalist world have broken with their previous *subordination* to the Russian model and Russian leadership—which does not mean that they have broken with Moscow. We are today witnessing the final phase of the long and complex historical trajectory of the "world party" of communism that was born out of the October revolution.

One of the constants of this trajectory has been that organisational and ideological monolithism has always concealed latent conflicts and forced them underground, so that even the participants could not follow their course. When any conflict finally broke to the surface, it was thus always in an unexpected and explosive form.

We may start from certain aspects of the theoretical conception held by Lenin in the years following October 1917 of "the world revolution" and the party that was destined to lead it. Proceeding from the assumption that capitalism was in its death-throes and that the European working classes were only awaiting the appearance of an "authentic revolutionary party" of the Bolshevik type to abandon their reformist leaders, Lenin considered that the immediate creation of such a party on a supranational *world* scale might be the decisive factor for the fate of the "world revolution"—a party rigorously organised and centralised on a planetary scale, under a semi-military discipline, with a supreme leadership to decide policy for each national section and control its application, select the local leaderships etc. In other words the exact opposite of the structure of the Second International. An added problem was that the omnipotent supreme body of this Third International was based in Moscow under the immediate control of the Russian party which was considered—at first tacitly and then officially—to be the "leading party".

This concept of "the world revolution and its party" was no sooner given a concrete structure than it came into contradiction with the real historical development of the West (and of the world in general)—the defeat of other attempts at revolution, the recovery of capitalism under various political guises, the renewal of social-democracy, the rise of fascism. The structures of the "world party" became an objective obstacle to the elaboration and application by Communists in each country of policies based on the real international context and their own national reality. Once Stalin was installed as dictator and the theory of "socialism in one country" officially adopted in the USSR, the contradiction became sharper. The Sixth Congress of the Communist International in 1928 enshrined the Soviet State as centre and base of the world revolution, to whose interests the activity of all Communist Parties must be unconditionally subordinated. Very soon the disastrous effects of this policy were reflected in the catastrophic defeat of the largest of the Comintern parties, the KPD, at the hands of Hitler.

It was in this period too that the first signs of theoretical and practical opposition appeared in the ranks of Communism, advocating different strategies from that imposed by Moscow. The platform and organisation of the "Left Opposition" (Trotskyism) quickly led to its expulsion. Gramsci, whose theoretical writings were ignored by the Communist movement for more than two decades, made an original analysis of the State and social structures of European capitalism and argued for the strategy for socialism which he called a "war of position". Mao developed his theory and practice of revolutionary war based on the peasantry as the appropriate strategy for agricultural countries colonised by imperialism where the proletariat was tiny—"the country laying siege to the city".

The quest by the USSR, after Hitler's seizure of power, for alliances with the capitalist democracies against the threat from Germany (1934–38) allowed the parties in those countries a greater degree of local initiative by way of the strategy of Popular Fronts. The experience of the Popular Fronts in France and Spain, however, showed how narrowly the local parties were still trammelled by the requirements of Soviet diplomacy, and in 1939 when the Soviet government suddenly switched from alliances against Hitler to an alliance with Hitler, all the Communist Parties had to change with it to the new position.

The second period of Soviet alliances with the capitalist democracies (1941–47) and the dissolution of the Comintern (1943) which this involved, again created the space for a limited autonomy for the Communist Parties. In both the Eastern countries that had been liberated by the Soviet armies and in the Western countries freed by the Anglo-American forces and the Resistance, there were efforts to elaborate pluralist democratic "national roads to socialism". Dimitrov and other leading Communists for the first time questioned whether the new revolutions would need to pass through a dictatorship of the proletariat (by which they understood the dictatorship of the Communist Party). Although these formulations were a response to real problems, they were fundamentally opportunist and essentially conditioned by the evolution of the "grand alliance" between the USSR and the USA and their division of the world into "zones of influence". The "national roads" of the West European parties reflected the subordination of their zone to bourgeois power and US dominance. In Eastern Europe a superficial pluralism concealed the fact that the Communist

Parties had effective control of the State apparatus, basing themselves not on the majority consent of the people, but on the Soviet armies that guaranteed Moscow's sway within their zone. Hence the end of the "grand alliance" swept away all the daring "innovations" in theory and practice of these parties overnight, once more exposing their unconditional subjection to Moscow. But each time resistances were growing.

The first task for the Cominform which was created in 1947 was to call the French and Italian parties to order for having taken too seriously the idea of a national road. The Yugoslav Communist Party, which had opposed Stalin in the same way—with the difference that they had the backing of an entire people with their own army, became the target for a hysterical campaign. In the "people's democracies" where the Communist Parties that had been hoisted to power by Soviet armies now found themselves under pressure on one side from the democratic demands of the population and on the other from the Kremlin's military-police apparatus, the growth of resistance was especially strong, and led to bloody purges affecting tens of thousands of militants and major leaders. The Cominform no longer provided Stalin with the same organisational means of compulsion over the Western parties that he had enjoyed under the Communist International—which no party of any standing had wished to see resurrected. Instead inherited ideology (reinforced a little by financial assistance) proved adequate to avoid any repetition of the Tito-Stalin split. But the tensions persisted, ready to erupt at any moment.

After the death of Stalin his successors sought to ease relations with the "fraternal parties" and the satellite states. In a series of spectacular concessions that changed little of substance there quickly followed: reconciliation with the Yugoslav party, denunciations of Stalin, winding up of Cominform, and renunciation by the Russians of their formal position as "leading party". In reality the Soviet leaders were seeking to reestablish their preminence in the international communist movement by these means. But these concessions marked the onset of another long period which has now brought us, after many twists and turns, to the present situation where (apart from the other members of the Soviet military bloc) every major party, East and West, has broken from subordination to the Soviet party. But before we examine that period, let us pick out a few other essential features of the process we have just described.

As the leadership of party and State in the USSR gradually changed in character, so the Soviet centre increased its organisational and ideological hold over the other Communist Parties, with ever worse effects. The party which had been revolutionary in the years immediately after October gradually came to be the expression of a new ruling class which had developed in the social system Stalin had built up in the course of industrialisation. The elimination of the initial Soviet democracy until nothing but the shell remained meant that the system could not properly be called socialist—nor even one of transition to socialism—since there was no longer any mechanism by which the workers might collectively master the means of production and manage social, economic and political institutions. (Obviously democracy at the point of production does not constitute a sufficient condition to ensure collective appropriation, but it is an absolutely necessary condition).

As this change progressed, the main motivation of foreign policy and relations with the other communist parties ceased to be "the advance of the revolution" and became "interests of State". The formula of "proletarian internationalism" became nothing more than an ideological justification for the way that the Kremlin manipulated the other parties in the interests of its own internal or external policy, even when this cut across a section's national policy. All the democratic content which the idea of "the dictatorship of the proletariat" had held for Marx was lost and it became a mystifying label for the dictatorship of the new class *over* the proletariat. The scientific rigour and critical revolutionary essence of Marx's thought was drained away, leaving "Marxism-Leninism" as the scholastic justification of the new class order. The Soviet leadership was quite unable, with this impoverished "Marxism", to theorise and transcend the contradictions we referred to at the start of this chapter between certain aspects of Comintern theory and organisation and the actions each party needed to take in its own country. On the contrary, Soviet *raison d'Etat* required the total instrumentalisation and subordination of the other parties.

According to the explanation most current among the Communist Parties, they did not succeed in developing adequate policies for their respective national class struggles because, after the defeat of initial attempts at revolution in Western Europe, they had to act as outposts of the isolated socialist fortress in the USSR, and everything else came second to its defence. There is an inconsistency in this explanation: would not the defence of the fortress have been better served by elaborating an appropriate line and carrying it through in the same way the Russians had done? In my opinion we have to look elsewhere for the real causes, as I have indicated above: they are to be found in (1) the strategy and organisational concept of the Comintern; (2) the increasing self-interest of the "fortress" which made it less internationalist, less Marxist, more concerned with the advancement of the new class—in a word, less socialist.

Why then did the Communist Parties not react against their subjection to this involuted Soviet regime? Many reasons can be advanced, but they can essentially be reduced to one; the colossal and durable impact of the October Revolution. For successive generations of revolutionaries (and still to some extent today) the Russian Revolution was a myth which made the exercise of critical judgment on any feature which did not fit the initial content of the myth impossible. The Communist Parties were unable to use that pseudo-Marxism in which they had been moulded almost from their inception as a tool for their own liberation—pseudo-Marxist because it was useless as an instrument for uncovering the reality behind appearances, serving only to "scientifically prove" that socialism was truly being built in the Soviet Union. In their defence of the USSR, Marxist purity and a monolithic unity of the party, they proceeded to eliminate every critical tendency which might have saved them.

Given their ideological blinkers (among which what might be called a "productivist" conception of socialism was, and remains, extremely important) and their own practice it was easy, almost inevitable, that the communists accepted as irrefutable proof of the socialist nature of the Soviet regime a series of facts that proved no such thing. True, there was a spectacular industrial development, broad masses of people were given access to culture, the USSR did play a decisive role in defeating the fascist powers and in aiding various revolutionary movements. The Communist Parties ignored the facts that the manner of industrialisation had produced new social antagonisms, and that the mass culture was imbued with an ideology that justified these new social relations and helped to reproduce and perpetuate them. They also failed to notice that the USSR's progressive international role could as well be explained by the fact that the new social order, although not socialist, was of a completely different type from Western capitalism and naturally generated contradictions and conflicts between the two (for although the USSR was also divided into classes of rulers and ruled, for it to revert to the same type as Western capitalism would have required the overthrow of the new ruling class and the transformation of the political and economic structures of the country). Great-power interests and the new ruling class's need for a "socialist" image as ideological legitimation also contributed to these conflicts.

The existence of concentration camps and show trials (first in the USSR, later in the peoples' democracies too), the monstrous repressive apparatus, the liquidation of soviet democracy—all were denied or camouflaged by the regime. Loyal Communists believed neither the denunciations from the Right nor the revelations of Trotsky and other revolutionaries (who were thereby excluded from the category). The individuals and small minority groups which did believe were immediately expelled. In the period from 1933 to the Second World War another factor helps to explain the blindness of Communists to what was going on in their own backyard—the threat of aggression by Hitler against "fortress Russia". Although some leading foreign Communists who lived in Moscow in those years had an inkling of what was happening and entertained some doubts, the combination of pressures we have mentioned made it either difficult to get to the bottom of the question or led them to stifle their doubts. Ernst Fischer's evidence in this respect is particularly eloquent.[11]

Those today, including some on the Left, who claim they cannot believe that Communists were ignorant of what was going on forget that social actions seldom appear with the clarity of incontrovertible truth. They are always perceived through the prism of subjectivity, ideology, partisan interests, historical conditioning—which is not to deny there were some cynics. The degree of "obviousness" of facts changes radically with historical distance.

From 1956 to the Eastern Scission

The mythology of Stalin and Soviet socialism was lent a new lustre by the role of the Soviet Union in the war against the fascist powers, when the entry of its armies into Eastern Europe initiated a revolutionary process which it at the same stroke distorted. It was only when, in order to safeguard the system by partial reform, the Soviet ruling class was itself obliged to draw back a little the veil which concealed Soviet reality, that the world's Communists were forced to yield to the evidence. All the revelations of communist "renegades" and capitalist propaganda machines were far surpassed by the reality. It became clear that effective power in the USSR had been not in the hands of the workers, but in those of an autocrat at the head of an unscrupulous totalitarian police apparatus (of which he was also, dialectically, the prisoner). It also became clear that there were surprising similarities between Moscow's relationship to the other countries

11. Ernst Fischer, *An Opposing Man*, London 1975.

of the "socialist camp" and the methods of imperialism.

The Communist Parties were profoundly shaken, although their ideological conditioning still persuaded the majority to accept the explanation of a "tumor in a healthy body". Nevertheless the CPSU's hegemony in the Communist movement was irredeemably compromised and centrifugal tendencies greatly strengthened. Moscow did not hesitate to unleash repression within the countries of the "socialist camp". Against the Poles in October 1956 the threat of armed intervention proved adequate; its exercise was needed to smash the workers' councils of Budapest. In both countries a large part if not a majority of the Communist party membership was involved in a popular rebellion directed as much against Russian domination as against the internal Stalinist regime.

Although Moscow was able to restore order in its European *glacis*, it had suffered a severe blow to its moral and political credit throughout the Communist movement. The Italian party alone lost 250,000 members, including many intellectuals, and a further 50,000 were lost by the other West European parties. In the leading groups of many parties serious disagreements arose, which were fuelled by two statements containing barely concealed criticisms of the Soviet leadership and its attempt to reduce the whole problem to the "cult of the personality". Mao in his theses on "contradictions among the people" argued that if the leadership of the revolution failed to implement policies that corresponded to the interests of the working class such contradictions could produce antagonism between party and people. Togliatti for his part aroused strong opposition within the leadership of the Italian party by his suggestion that Communists should seek an explanation of Stalinism in contradictions of the Russian system.

But if the events of 1956 and the loss of membership aroused demands for more discussion and a new critical spirit, they also scared the party leaderships, including those that were most ready for an opening. The "Hundred Flowers" campaign was cut short in China and Togliatti moderated his initial reaction. By November 1957 Moscow was able to take advantage of the lull to organise the first world congress of Communist Parties since the dissolution of the Comintern. Mao attended and made common cause with the Soviet party in the battle against "revisionism'—Yugoslav "revisionism" again serving as the scapegoat so the ranks could be closed against every tendency to autonomy or critical thought.

Moscow managed to restore something of its authority, even Mao advising that the Soviet party's leading role should be accepted. However by the time the second world conference met three years later in 1960, this temporary alliance between the two communist "big powers" had given way to major differences. The Chinese rejected Moscow's interpretation of "peaceful coexistence" and, through the mouth of the Albanians, accused them of capitulating to imperialism. The great majority of the conference backed the Soviet party, accusing the Chinese, Albanians and others in return of "Left deviationism". As with the 1957 meeting, the debates were not published, but a compromise resolution was adopted which concealed the serious differences behind triumphalist assertions: "All the speculations by imperialists, renegades and revisionists of a scission in the socialist camp are built on sand and are bound to fail. All socialist countries regard the unity of the socialist camp as the apple of their eye."[12]

A year later the first broadsides of the great schism were published.

At the 22nd congress of the CPSU in November 1961 Khruschev, under pressure from the power struggles within the Soviet leadership, again denounced the bloody repression of the Stalin era, furnishing new information. The combination of the Stalin question and the Sino-Soviet polemic led to tensions and differences in the leading bodies of many Communists Parties. Majority opinion in the French and Spanish parties considered Khruschev's policies to be an adequate guarantee of destalinisation and a democratisation of

12. Statement issued by the Conference of Communist and Workers' Parties, Moscow, November 1960.

the Soviet regime. But the Italian leadership demanded "additional explanations, because the denunciations of the Stalin era also pose the problem of the responsibility of the Italian and other parties"; they asked for a thorough investigation into the situation in the Communist movement under Stalin and again proposed "full autonomy for each party".[13]

The CPSU now for the first time in its history faced a rival which was its match on every level—politically, ideologically, in state and military terms. The Maoist "anti-revisionist" theses were of course directed equally against the West European parties, particularly the Italian. Chinese incomprehension of the problems facing the class struggle in the advanced capitalist countries, combined with the ambiguity of Mao's position over Stalinism, at first led the French and Spanish parties to take Moscow's side unconditionally and to launch ill-considered attacks on the Chinese. Overall, however, the effect of the Sino-Soviet split was to stimulate centrifugal tendencies. The same was to be true of Khruschev's fall in 1964. The demise of his colourful personality had a traumatic effect on the leaders of some parties who had seen in him the personification of their hopes for democratisation of the Soviet system. In 1966 (with the trial and sentencing of the writers Sinyafsky and Daniel) the French and Spanish parties for the first time joined the Italians in open criticism of an instance of cultural-political repression in Russia.

In the long decade following Stalin's death the West European parties started once again to explore their own roads to socialism. In the Third World countries there were similar efforts in relation to the anti-imperialist national liberation struggles. In Latin America the experience of Cuba, generally poorly assimilated, led to the adoption of a guerilla road; in many Asian countries the Chinese experience inspired versions of people's war. Nearly every party faced some kind of crisis, either Maoist or Castroist splits or (as in Spain in 1964) an internal crisis of the leadership. Trotskyism once more won a certain audience. The theoretical impotence of Moscow's authorised version of Marxism-Leninism, which still

13. Statement by the leadership of the PCI issued 27 November 1961.

held sway in most of the Communist Parties, blocked the objective need to develop new strategies and to account for new phenomena within capitalism and imperialism, and within the "socialist camp". When these objective pressures produced a certain renaissance of Marxism, it occurred mainly outside the Communist Parties—if not in opposition to them—but increasingly involved militants within them. New debates developed between the various interpretations of Marxism propounded by existentialists, structuralists, historicists and others.

The advent of the Cultural Revolution in China for the first time suggested the possibility—although a very rudimentary one—of an overall alternative to the Soviet model. Most of the present leaders of the Eurocommunist parties stubbornly opposed this movement of renewal until one by one, without any critical review of their previous line, they retreated and then tried opportunistically to accommodate themselves to it.

The sum of these phenomena make it clear that, far from having overcome the elements of crisis that had already been apparent in "the world party" which preceded it, the "communist movement" had now entered a *general crisis*. From the dissolution of the Comintern—symbolising the crisis of "the world party"—to the first major split with the Eastern schism, a steady decomposition of the "movement" had been occurring, poorly concealed by ever more formal diplomatic links between the parties. The hegemony of the Soviet party within the movement was now largely a fiction, maintained by the ruling parties in the East European satellite states and a host of parties in Latin America, Africa and the Middle East which had little or no weight in their own countries and could scarcely have survived without Moscow's financial aid. By the mid-1960s it was clear that there was a radical contradiction between the objective necessities—ideological, political and organisational—of the struggle for socialism in the advanced capitalist countries and the Third World, and the scholastic Marxism-Leninism of a Soviet party-state whose internal and external policies were based on the interests of its new ruling class. From 1968 the contradiction became politically acute.

No Possible "Normalisation"

1968 marked a crucial moment in the evolution of the communist movement in Western Europe, particularly for the three big parties with which this essay is mainly concerned. The prospect of socialist revolution in the mature capitalist countries was given a new immediacy by the great social explosion in France that May, while the "Prague spring" created a similar prospect for the Eastern countries. Let us look first at the events in Czechoslovakia.

Confirming the lessons of the Polish October and the Hungarian rising of 1956, the Czech spring demonstrated once more that any road to socialism in the countries cast in the "Soviet mould" must involve a break with their characteristic social and political structures—in other words, a new revolution. It was equally clear that in those countries where the Communist Parties were in power the contradictions ran right down the middle of the party—a matter of considerable importance in anticipating any such new revolution. The defeat of the Czech venture did not remove its social causes; both there and in Poland, Hungary and the other satellite states, the new repressions and the passage of time were preparing the ground for new crises.

Moscow's military intervention proved beyond any doubt that the regime erected by Stalin and consolidated by his successors was quite incompatible with *real*—that is to say democratic—socialism. The West European parties which had been evolving in the way we have described faced a difficult choice. If they approved the invasion of little democratic socialist Czechoslovakia their avowals of faith in freedom and democracy would lose all credibility. For the first time in their history they dared to express public disagreement with an action by the CPSU that condensed the very nature of the Soviet party. It was an important step, but not decisive; although these parties did not accept—as they had in the case of Hungary in 1956—that Moscow's action could be justified in the defence of socialism, they still held that the Soviet regime was basically socialist. The Soviet party had made a grave error, but that did not put the nature of the Russian regime into question. It was a form of socialism that would not be acceptable in the Western countries, but socialism none the less. There was therefore no question of a break with the CPSU; what was needed was moderate criticism and the restoration of unity in the communist movement on the basis of full acknowledgment for the right of each Communist Party to choose its own road. Although this position was not accepted by the Russians, it did leave room for a compromise so that the third conference of the world's Communist parties could be convened in June 1969.

The Chinese and their allies had originally requested the meeting in 1962 in order to provoke a general debate about the differences. The Soviet party soon adopted the project in the hope of getting a majority to condemn the Chinese, and thereby to restore its own authority. This move in turn was resisted by the Italian and other parties. Shortly before his death in the summer of 1964, Togliatti had addressed a document—the so-called "Yalta memorial"—to the leadership of the CPSU, in which he made a number of criticisms of the state of political and cultural freedom in the USSR and also expressed his opposition to the Soviet plan for a world conference; he proposed instead that the communist movement should accept a "unity in diversity" which should include the Chinese.

After several years of argument and some concessions by the Russians, the meeting was agreed for the end of 1968. The invasion of Czechoslovakia meant that it had to be postponed, but made the Soviet Union even more determined to prove to the peoples of the Soviet bloc and to world opinion that it had the support of the great majority of the communist movement. Having proceeded in the name of "normalisation" to a classical Stalinist purge of the Czech party—half a million communists expelled from the party, the leadership imprisoned, banished or driven into exile—Moscow now proposed to "normalise" the entire movement and restore its hegemony. Pressure on the "difficult" parties was increased, confronting them with the dilemma of surrender or risk of a major confrontation, for which few of their members were prepared and which would have been difficult for them to reconcile with their continued acceptance of the East European regimes as socialist. Since the Kremlin had no interest in such a break either, a compromise was eventually reached whereby neither China nor Czechoslovakia would be mentioned in the preparatory document or in the final resolution; but each party could express its own positions in the proceedings, which would be published.

The Soviet party and its loyal supporters used the conference as a platform to launch a formal offensive against the Chinese and to win support for the "normalisation" of Czechoslovakia and the Brezhnev doctrine of "limited sovereignty" (the right for any "socialist country" to intervene in another if "socialism" is at risk). The main West European parties, plus the Rumanians, Japanese and a few others, maintained their criticisms and reaffirmed the right of each party independently to develop and apply their own policies. The Spanish delegation affirmed that democratic centralism could not be applied to relations between parties—something which was only too evident in the conduct of the conference itself. The most lucid and rounded exposition of the line of opposition which has since developed into Eurocommunism was provided by Berlinguer. The Italian delegation also refused to sign the conference document because there was no explicit agreement that alternative "models" of socialism could exist. Three other parties which did sign—those of Spain, Rumania and Switzerland —expressed major reservations about its general content.

Only 60 parties—21 less than at the previous conference in 1960—signed the text without explicit objections, and these included the French, Japanese and other parties that had advanced different positions of their own in the conference, albeit not so vigorously as the Italians and the Spanish.

Another noteworthy case was the Australian party, small but influential in the trade unions, which made one of the toughest criticisms of the invasion of Czechoslovakia. The parties of China, Vietnam, North Korea, Yugoslavia, Albania and Holland had refused to attend, and it should also be noted that some of the pro-Soviet parties present—such as those of India, Greece and Israel—coexist with other organisations of a similar or greater weight in their own countries that are independent of Moscow.

In short the conference—taking into account what was said and what was left unsaid, those who attended and those who stayed away—presented a picture of an international Communist movement wracked by a general structural and ideological crisis. But it also showed that the Soviet Party was prepared to battle against the tide and that the opposition was apprehensive of going any further. Some of the "opposition", such as the French party, were only too eager to accept "normalisation" with Moscow on the basis of mutual independence and non-interference, even if that meant tacitly accepting the "normalisation" of Czechoslovakia—the bloodiest example of interference in the affairs of a "fraternal party", or keeping quiet about the persecution of the leading figures of the "Prague spring".

None of the parties that had dared to resist Moscow was able to break the umbilical cord that linked them to Eastern "socialism" and take their criticisms to their logical conclusion. The degree of opposition varied from one country to another; in all of them a large proportion of the membership and many of the leaders of the party were still marked by the Stalinism and Soviet mythology of their formative years. A few individuals who had broken the cord were now asking whether the Czech affair did not put in question the very nature of the USSR and its associated states. Although they did not all take the same position, they included Garaudy from the French leadership; Fischer, Marek and other top leaders of the Austrian party; and the *Manifesto* group within the PCI. Moscow demanded that their parties take stern measures against these flagrant examples of "anti-sovietism", and at the same time gave encouragement and assistance to pro-Soviet elements in each party which were making the same charge against their own leaderships.

Each leadership determined its own attitude at the 1969 conference and in the subsequent period according to its particular circumstances. Their historical experience enabled the Italian party and leadership to resist the unprecedented Soviet attacks best. Although the CPSU took some comfort from the expulsion of the *Manifesto* group, this only occurred after their positions had been fully developed in debate before the entire party, allowing the leadership to make use of their Left critiques of Soviet "socialism" to strengthen their resistance to Moscow's pressure for "normalisation".

In the PCF both party and leadership were more strongly marked by their Stalinist background; the leading group retreated from its original positions more readily than the Italians. It did not withdraw their condemnation of the invasion, but simply discouraged further discussion of the subject and used the Garaudy affair to revive all the traditional arguments against "anti-Soviet activity". The PCF made much of material achievements in the Soviet Union, and of its supposedly decisive anti-imperialist role; it took a complacent attitude to the Czech "normalisation" and redoubled its attacks on Maoism. Indeed the main cause of friction between the French party and Moscow at this period was the latter's praise of French foreign policy which went so far as an approval by the Soviet ambassador of the candidature of Giscard on the eve of the 1974 presidential election.

Prior to the Czech crisis the Spanish party had a reputation as one of the more pro-Soviet parties. In practice its attitude had begun to change with the fall of Khruschev, when they had just expelled those of us who had taken positions critical of the Soviet system. It was clear that the policy of broad alliances against the dictatorship, in the struggle for democracy in Spain was incompatible with any lauding of East European "socialism". The PCE therefore naturally welcomed Dubcek's "new course" and reacted angrily to the invasion. The party organ *Mundo Obrero* immediately responded: "We find inconceivable and unacceptable the situation which our enemies now claim would apply—that from the first day when our party, in alliance with the forces of labour and culture, comes to power in Spain, any other socialist power should be in a position to dictate our policy or even to intervene militarily against our territory—we resist this most energetically."[14]

Shortly afterwards Carrillo reported to the Central Committee that "a kind of cold war" now existed "within our own camp". He laid all responsibility for the grave situation in the Communist movement on "the policies of those parties which are in power", which he declared were determined by "reasons of state". He rejected the argument that the invasion had been necessary to protect the Soviet zone of influence and the *status quo*: "We reject such a concept, which may correspond to their notion of their own State interests, but has nothing in common with a class position". He posed the need for a deeper examination of the roots of Stalinism and the successive "crises in the development of Socialism" and warned against any "attempt against the unity of our party".[15] This last warning was directly aimed at the Soviet Party for the assistance they had been giving to Eduardo Garcia (organisation secretary) and the eight other members of the Executive Committee or Central Committee who had already launched a struggle within the party around the banner of loyalty to the Soviet Union (and who would be joined a year later by Enrique Lister).

This struggle within the Spanish party took a particularly vicious form in the USSR and the other East European countries where important groups of exiled militants were open to the pressure of Soviet agents. The PCE leadership and Santiago Carrillo in particular were faced with a choice between surrender or an all-out fight. The PCE took the clearest stand against the Czech "normalisation" of any of

14. *Mundo Obrero*, September 1968.
15. Report to the Central Committee, published as a pamphlet September 1968, PCE.

the West European parties—although it still launched no systematic campaign. In 1970 *Mundo Obrero*, protesting Dubcek's expulsion from the party, declared that "even expelled he remains a hope for the future of Czech socialism". It also denounced the gradual restoration of diplomatic relations with the Francoist regime by the "socialist countries".[16]

In September 1973 the PCE published a report by Manuel Azcárate (responsible for international relations in the party) to the Central Committee which systematised the party's criticisms of Soviet policy. While expressing certain criticisms of Peking's foreign policy, it dismissed as "nonsense" the proposal by the Soviet Union and other East European states to condemn China before the Committee of the Assembly of Public Opinion for European Security which met in Brussels in May of that year. It denounced the tendency of Soviet international policy to accept the social and political *status quo*: "in its foreign policy", declared Azcárate, "the revolution has sunk beyond the horizon." The report proposed that the West European Communist Parties should jointly struggle for an independent democratic Europe "free from the hegemony of any great power". The idea of a new world conference of communist parties which the leaders of Bulgaria, East Germany and Czechoslovakia had recently been putting forward on behalf of Brezhnev, was opposed on the grounds that it was intended to restore unconditional subservience to the CPSU. Azcárate countered this proposal with a plan to strengthen links between the West European parties, to develop a common strategy and a clear "brand image" of the kind of socialism they wanted for the region. After some marginal criticisms of the lack of democracy in the East European regimes, he concluded that the root of their problems was the dominant role of the State and the fusion of Party and State.

When the CPSU replied harshly in one of their publications, the PCE responded by publishing the original report together with the Soviet reply and its reply to the letter,

16. *Mundo Obrero*, no. 13, 1970.

together with an introduction confirming that the report represented the views of the Central Committee.[17]

In spite of temporising by the PCF and (to a lesser extent) the PCI, the main areas of contention persisted and became more severe. The two parties joined with the Spanish in stubbornly refusing to grant the Russian Party a new world conference. The links between these three and the other West European parties were strengthened, and in January 1974 there occurred the meeting which some observers were to see as marking the birth of a new "West-European Communism".

Each of the three parties was now developing a national strategy—the "Common Programme" in France, the "Historic Compromise" in Italy, the "Pact for Freedom" in Spain—in a context of increasing opportunity for the Left, which required that they clearly differentiate themselves from the Soviet "model". They had already combined in 1971 to criticise the trial of a group of Jews in Leningrad who wanted to leave the USSR, and in 1973 when the Russians refused to publish the works of Solzhenitsyn. In 1975 they jointly protested the internment of the mathematician Leonid Plyusch in a psychiatric hospital, and in May that year the PCF published a draft "declaration of rights" which was intended to remove any doubts about its relationship to the East European regimes.

This series of actions could sometimes be contradicted by other attitudes in the same parties—during much of this period for example the French party was supporting the policies of the very pro-Soviet Portuguese Communist Party. But the general dynamic of the course taken by the three major West European parties was to deepen the rift with Moscow and frustrate the Soviet plan for "normalisation". In the course of 1976 that tendency reached a critical point.

Towards a Western Schism?

In autumn 1974 the Soviet Party gave in: instead of a world

17. Undated pamphlet issued by the PCE, approximately March or April 1974.

conference, it would be a "pan-European" one, comprising the parties of East and West Europe. The consultative meeting in Warsaw in October 1974 had decided that it should take place by mid-1975 at the latest, but from the first preparatory meetings the opposing tendencies were in dispute and it was not finally convened until June 1976.

In the declaration of Livorno, issued by the PCI and PCE in July 1975, and the Rome declaration of the PCI and the PCF in November 1975 the three West European parties provided the clearest statement to date of their strategy and their concept of socialism. The second was especially significant because it showed that—apart from some major tactical differences over NATO and the EEC—the French Party was now almost completely aligned on the traditional Italian positions.

We shall refer again to these basic documents of Eurocommunism later (the term first appears following the Rome declaration). For the moment it is enough to register that the three parties made it plain in a way they had not done previously that they had a *common* conception of socialism and the transition which was quite incompatible with the East European regimes, and in so doing took a further decisive step along the path of confrontation with Moscow.

From that moment the process accelerated. Although the events are still quite recent, we will briefly recapitulate them. French television screened a film, shot in secret, which included pictures of political prisoners in a Soviet "labour camp". The leadership of the PCF reacted immediately by declaring that if there was no public denial by the Soviet authorities "it would express the deepest surprise (sic) and strongest disapproval of such unjustifiable acts" because the PCF "was against any curtailment of human rights and especially of freedom of opinion, expression and pub-lication". Moscow responded by accusing the PCF in the pages of *Pravda* "whether intentionally or not of instigating new anti-soviet acts".[18] The leaders of the French party

18. The communiqué of the PCF Political Bureau was published in *L'Humanité* 13 December 1975. The CPSU's reply appeared in *Pravda* 19 December 1975.

restated their position; for the first time in their entire history they proceeded to a general acknowledgment and condemnation of political repression in the Soviet Union. The Italian and Spanish parties took similar positions, the PCE taking the opportunity to add that the situation in Czechoslovakia since 1968 "constitutes the negation of every basic socialist principle".[19]

In the course of preparations for their 22nd Congress (in February 1976) the general secretary of the French Party announced that he was in favour of dropping the formula "dictatorship of the proletariat". Although from a Marxist point of view the manner and justification of this abandonment were unacceptable, in context it signified a rejection of the theoretical and practical content acquired by the formula in the history of the Soviet regime. The parties of Spain, Italy and other countries had "let it drop" with as little noise as possible years before. Proceeding in a more spectacular fashion, the PCF sought to compensate for its tardiness by sensationalism, in this as in other unorthodox departures. It went on to repudiate the notion of "socialist internationalism" which Moscow had concocted as a higher category than "proletarian internationalism" to describe the bonds that united the parties and states of the Soviet bloc—and which provided a spurious pseudo-Marxist basis for the doctrine of "limited sovereignty" that had been used to justify the intervention against Czechoslovakia and other possible future cases. Carrillo, for his part, argued that "proletarian internationalism" was an outdated concept, partly because it provided cover for Soviet hegemony, but also because it was too restrictive for the present stage of struggle against imperialism.

Two weeks after the PCF's 22nd Congress, the 25th Congress of the CPSU was held. Brezhnev with his subalterns from the Soviet party and the faithful from the other parties counter-attacked all along the line, charging the Eurocommunists with "nationalism", "revisionism", and "opportunism". Zhivkov, head of the Bulgarian Party and State,

19. *Informaciones del PCE* no. 2, January 1976.

accused them of breaching the principle of principles: "It is the attitude they show towards the USSR which is the very touchstone of revolutionaries and internationalists, the line that divides the forces of progress from the forces of reaction".[20] Brezhnev and his followers scarcely referred to the Pan-European conference which was in preparation, but instead insisted on the need for a new world conference which would provide them with a better arithmetical balance of forces to do battle with Eurocommunism and Maoism.

In an unprecedented gesture for general secretaries of their rank Marchais and Carrillo stayed away from the CPSU congress. Berlinguer attended only to expound his party's line from the platform. Carrillo in fact joined in the "debate" in his own way from Rome with a reference to "the primitive condition of Soviet socialism which still bears the marks of the near feudal system which it destroyed".[21] *L'Humanité* took pains to call attention to the lavish tributes to "the personality" of Brezhnev at the conference.

On 17 March, as the conference neared its close, Suslov launched an attack on the Eurocommunists, still without naming them. The Manichean version of their ideological positions attributed to them in his speech was condemned out of court. Their abandonment of the "dictatorship of the proletariat" and of "proletarian internationalism" became "the substitution of bourgeois liberalism for Marxism" and "a service to the class enemy". The search for a new road to socialism was dismissed with these words: "what the opportunists would have us accept as national or regional variations of Marxism have nothing in common with revolutionary theory and are an attack on the working class".[22] The Eurocommunist press, of course, flatly rejected these accusations.

Various other Eastern-bloc notables followed Suslov, with the Czechs taking the prize for speeches whose ardour of pro-Soviet sentiments was in inverse proportion to their

20. *Le Monde*, 28 February 1976.
21. ibid.
22. *Le Monde*, 19 March 1976.

popular support. Vasili Bilak declared that "Soviet Communism provides us with the best model", while Josef Kempis sounded the alarm against "those who claim to be Marxists but in reality are directed by the subversive agencies of imperialism".[23] Meanwhile, a pamphlet was appearing in the USSR attacking Luciano Gruppi, head of the PCI's cultural commission. In its reply the Italian party daily *L'Unità* retorted that the author's "grotesque lucubrations" had twisted Lenin's thought into "a system of immutable dogma" and that the attack on Gruppi was really directed "against the fundamental policy choices of the PCI and other Western parties."[24] The offensive against Eurocommunism continued at the Congress of the East German United Socialist Party (Communist Party) in May—but there is no need for us to enumerate every step of the campaign of the months following the CPSU congress.

Fearful of the effect that a complete schism with the Western parties would have on their own parties and peoples, Moscow and its partners of the Eastern bloc all turned up for the Pan-European conference in East Berlin on 29 June 1976. Four days before the conference started, Polish workers—this time with the backing of many intellectuals—had again exploded in anger against the anti-working-class policies of their regime. Representatives of the Prague spring had also written to the West European parties from their prisons or from exile asking for solidarity. Brezhnev and his lieutenants had been aware that in coming to the conference they ran some risk of an open declaration from the Eurocommunists, but they got more than they had bargained for. Even in the text of the agreed document it was obvious that the Soviets were forced to make major concessions. Four of the holy tenets of Marxist orthodoxy were missing—there was no "Marxism-Leninism", no "dictatorship of the proletariat", no "proletarian internationalism", and no "struggle against anti-sovietism". Instead there were to be found formulas to which Moscow was known to be hostile: the

23. *La Vanguardia*, Barcelona, 21 March 1976.
24. *Le Monde*, 21–22 March 1976.

Italian formula of "international solidarity" replaced "proletarian internationalism"; instead of the Stalinist invention of "Marxism-Leninism", the parties were to develop "basing themselves on the great ideas of Marx, Engels and Lenin, but strictly preserving the equality and sovereign independence of each party, non-interference in each other's internal affairs and freedom to choose their different roads in the struggle for progressive social change and for socialism."[25] The bulk of the document concentrated on questions of peace and coexistence where agreement was easier—although in speeches by the Eurocommunists there were some indirect but transparent criticisms of certain aspects of Soviet foreign policy.

The Eurocommunists set the tone of the conference with a plain, occasionally blunt exposition of their politics. "Once Moscow was our Rome," declared Carrillo,[26] "but no more. Now we acknowledge no guiding centre, no international discipline . . . We could not accept any return to the concepts or structures proper to a previous period of internationalism". He numbered among "the greatest dangers that threaten us today", both "imperialist ambitions" and "the drive for hegemony". It was necessary "to accept once and for all the diversity of our movement, and to renounce any attempt to intrigue against it." He demanded of the "socialist countries, a more adventurous policy, to appeal before all the peoples of the world for the withdrawal of troops and bases from all foreign countries, socialist or capitalist; for the dismantling of the two existing military blocs; for effective guarantees of human rights in their broadest interpretation."

Carrillo, Marchais and Berlinguer all repeated that socialism, freedom and democracy are mutually dependent. Berlinguer provided such a detailed, concrete description of what he meant by freedom and democracy that it is difficult to

25. L'Humanité, 3 July 1976.
26. Quotations from speeches made at the Berlin conference taken from: L'Humanité, 1 July 1976 for Marchais, L'Unità, 1 July 1976 for Berlinguer, and from a duplicated text made available by the PCE delegation for Carrillo.

understand, from his speech, how he could still regard what obtains in the so-called socialist countries as falling within the category of socialism—even as a primitive variety. But of course Eurocommunism has still to resolve this not insignificant contradiction.

Marchais insisted that "peaceful coexistence should in no way be identified with an acceptance of the *status quo* in our country, nor with the division of the world into spheres of influence under the domination of the more powerful states." Referring directly to Moscow's repeated lauding of Giscard d'Estaing's foreign policy, the General Secretary of the French Party warned that "we can in no way accept that our struggle against the power of big capital, for democracy and socialism, should suffer in the name of peaceful coexistence between states." Berlinguer too stressed that *détente* must not imply "the maintenance in every country of the old social and political equilibrium", but according to him the break-up of the blocs should be achieved "gradually, without any unilateral change in the strategic balance between the North Atlantic Treaty and the Warsaw Pact." The Italian people should decide their own destiny independently, but "within the framework of the international alliances to which Italy belongs". (We shall refer later to the foreign policy differences among the Eurocommunist parties.) Marchais and Berlinguer also criticised the traditional style of Communist Conferences (including the present one) and proposed a new, more direct and frank discussion of problems—thus aborting the Soviet plan to use the Pan-European conference as a springboard from which to prepare a new world conference.

Although they still did not wholly accept the term, by their interventions the three party leaders in fact confirmed the reality of Eurocommunism. For they did not merely agree on all essential questions, they also openly acknowledged that agreement. In Berlinguer's words "It is significant that several of the Communist and Workers' parties of Western Europe have arrived, by way of independent investigations, at similar conclusions about the road to socialism and the nature of the socialist society they wish to construct in their countries. These common features and convergences of opinion were recently expressed in the declarations which we made jointly with the comrades of the Communist parties of Spain, France and Great Britain." He also (as we already saw at the beginning of this work) underlined that the speed with which the term "Eurocommunism" had caught on indicated the depth of the need felt in Western Europe to discover new solutions to the problems of socialism.

In short, the Berlin conference provided the first all-round public confrontation between the Soviet bloc and Eurocommunism. It was now possible to see more clearly the likelihood of a Western schism in the Communist movement. For in spite of greater candour, these public discussions only partly reflected the depths of the conflict.

After the Berlin Conference the clashes grew daily worse. They now tended to centre on the most obviously anti-popular aspects of the East European regimes: their repression of every demand for freedom, and especially drastic repression of any demand for freedom linked to a struggle for working-class rights, as in the events of June 1976 in Poland. The PCI wrote to the Central Committee of the Polish party to intercede on behalf of the persecuted workers and on the same day the Italian press published Jacek Kuron's letter to Berlinguer. In it he asked for assistance "for the Polish workers who have been slandered by the press, radio and television, beaten by the police, locked up, charged with sabotage and sentenced to long terms of imprisonment."[27] French and Italian trade unions also expressed solidarity with the Polish workers. In December (a little late in the day) one of the secretaries of the CGT stated that "We find it unacceptable that workers should be given long prison sentences for going on strike, as happened some months ago in Poland".[28] In October Pierre Juquin, a member of the Central Committee, was sent to represent the PCF at a meeting in the Mutualité called to demand the freedom of a group of political prisoners in the USSR, Czechoslovakia, Bolivia, Chile and Uruguay.

27. Le Monde, 21 July 1976.
28. Le Monde, 30 December 1976.

(Only a year before the PCF had refused to take part in a meeting organised by the same "committee of mathematicians" for Leonid Plyusch—though they had made their own separate call for the Ukrainian mathematician to be freed). Moscow was outraged. Tass reported that "Soviet public opinion is unable to comprehend how representatives of the French party could be involved in such a dirty business . . . which is just intended to raise a wave of hostile propaganda against the Soviet Union and the other socialist countries and to strike a blow against international *détente*".[29] Marchais replied that the PCF was doing no more than applying the line adopted at their 22nd Congress "from which we shall not depart by one iota for anybody"; *L'Humanité* reaffirmed "the indivisibility of freedom and socialism",[30] and the PCF published six million copies of Juquin's speech.

In November it was East Germany's turn to provoke Eurocommunist protests when the GDR deprived the dissident singer Wolf Biermann of his nationality while he was on tour in West Germany, and launched a new wave of repression against the intellectual opposition. In December French television screened *L'Aveu*, a film account of the tragic show trials of the Stalin era, and the PCF sent Kanapa to represent it in the television debate which followed—the functionary responsible for the party's international relations, who until recently was himself a thorough-going Stalinist. When the film had appeared in the cinema in 1970, *L'Humanité* had described it as "serving an evil cause". Now Kanapa gave it his unreserved approval, declaring it "completely authentic" and claiming that the book from which it had been taken "has been of service to all who fight for socialism".[31]

Rude Pravo, the organ of the "normalised" Czech Communist Party, promptly denounced the French broadcast as "a provocation against Communism and against Czechoslovakia".[32] The editor-in-chief of *L'Humanité* replied that

29. *Le Monde*, 24 October 1976.
30. *L'Humanité*, 23 October 1976.
31. *Le Monde*, 16 December 1976.
32. *Le Monde*, 17 December 1976.

58

although we may no longer be in the same era as the show-trials of Prague or Moscow, nevertheless "attacks on individual liberty" persist, and "we have declared our opposition to such attacks and shall do so again whenever we consider it necessary . . . we shall never tolerate injustice for reasons of state."[33] *L'Unita* described the accusation as "a direct attack" and "a grave matter".[34]

In December Zhivkov, the leader of the Bulgarian Party who makes a speciality of saying plainly what Brezhnev prefers to say circumspectly, accused Eurocommunism of being "a new form of anti-Sovietism." Shortly afterwards occurred the famous exchange of prisoners between Brezhnev and Pinochet at Zurich—Corvalán for Bukovsky. Marchais called it "an unacceptable trade" and the PCF Political Bureau declared that it was impermissible that "a man who has fought for his idea of justice should have to face the intolerable choice between exile and imprisonment".[35] For *L'Unità* "the real problem lies in the evident restrictions of freedom in the USSR . . . This is the question which must now be openly discussed, clearly faced and resolved. The detention of people for so-called crimes of opinion is quite unacceptable, as is any other form of restriction on individual or collective liberties . . . The USSR could and should have realised by now how heavily all these unresolved problems about liberties weigh on its internal life."[36] Within a few days the Kremlin had responded with further arrests—of some Jews who had tried to demonstrate in the centre of Moscow, and of a group of Leningrad intellectuals accused of having painted on the walls of the Peter-Paul fortress an enormous slogan: "Though you strangle liberty, the people's spirit accepts no restraint".

In the first days of January 1977 a document was distributed in Czechoslovakia, signed by more than a hundred major political and intellectual figures, many of whom had played an important role in the movement of 1968. *Charter*

33. ibid.
34. *Le Monde*, 5–6 December 1976.
35. *L'Humanité*, 18 December 1976.
36. *L'Unità*, 18 December 1976.

77 denounced the lack of fundamental rights and freedoms, invoking the Helsinki agreements which the Czech government had signed, to demand that they be restored. Its signatories declared themselves to be a broad movement with no formal structure, directed to this one goal. In spite of a new wave of repression there was a positive response in the country and more signatures were added. The Eurocommunist parties expressed their solidarity, though without great enthusiasm. In Spain the PCE published the Charter document with an introduction by the Central Committee's Press Secretariat which described the document as representative of "a commitment still widespread in the whole of Czech society to the difficult task of constructing a socialism with a human face, (a task) in which they can count on the support of all democrats and socialists, Spanish Communists foremost among them." *L'Humanité* on 25 January denounced "the way in which the Czech authorities have dealt with political and intellectual figures who express opinions that differ from official standpoints . . . (Such behaviour) causes French Communists grave concern . . . we cannot forbear to express our stupefaction at the claim of the Czech authorities in *Rude Pravo* that the signatories of *Charter 77* were acting 'under the orders of anti-communist and Zionist agencies'. The use of such methods inevitably recalls the arbitrary acts of a dramatic past, any return to which would be unhesitatingly condemned by the French Communists." In spite of repression against the signatories—loss of jobs, detentions, interrogations, slanderous campaigns in the press—support for *Charter 77* grew throughout the country. In February, in response to the official campaign of denigration, Jiri Hajek gave an interview on Austrian television. One of the most distinguished signatories, a former Foreign Minister, he stated that the Charter aimed "to develop the Czech system of socialism further in the direction of democracy and humanism . . . and to contribute to the progress of *détente* throughout Europe". According to Hajek "those of us who have been excluded from the party but still consider ourselves communists and part of the international communist movement

intend by this initiative to contribute as citizens to the realisation of that goal."

Parallel with this development, the activity of the Workers' Defence Committee in Poland forced the government to ease up its repression and to promise an amnesty. The Committee insistently called for solidarity from the Communist and Socialist parties in the West, and sought to work out a political strategy. In the USSR there was also an increase in the activity of the various committees created to press that the Helsinki agreements (on human rights) be honoured; while exiles like Plyusch, Bielocherkovsky, Bukovsky and Amalrik intensified their work toward the same end and also tried to establish a basis for unified political action by all democratic socialists opposed to the Soviet dictatorship. Marchais made the gesture of holding a television discussion with Amalrik. Other officials from the French, Italian and Spanish Communist Parties established contact with exiles from the various East European countries. The authorities in those countries, and especially in the Soviet Union, reacted with increased repression and direct and indirect attacks on Eurocommunism. The ideological offensive was intensified after the meeting of Soviet-bloc parties in Sofia, which was timed to coincide with the Eurocommunist "summit" of the PCI, PCF and PCE in Madrid. The Madrid conference proved to be something of a damp squib, producing no further critique of the East European regimes, no denunciation of the increase in repression, no gesture of solidarity towards its victims—only a confirmation of previously stated positions.

The Key Question—The Nature of the System

The Eurocommunist parties have now reached a point from which they cannot retreat without losing credibility with their own membership and public opinion in their own countries. On the one hand they affirm the interdependence of socialism, freedom and democracy—while on the other they continue to regard the East European regimes as socialist in spite of increasingly sharp denunciations of their lack of freedom, which it becomes ever more difficult to dismiss simply as exceptions or mistakes. The logical conclusion of their denunciations is that these are not anomalies, but the natural product of a socio-political system in which freedom and democracy are conspicuous by their absence. But if the Eurocommunists were to arrive at that conclusion, to which they are already very close, how could they still justify their acceptance of it as socialist? To refer to "primitive socialism" is a mere subterfuge when it has been in existence for sixty years and has achieved such a high level of industrialisation. Even if we discount the matter of duration and industrialisation (the latter cannot, as we have said, by itself be taken to constitute evidence of socialism), a "primitive socialism" would at least have to show some signs of a dynamic progress towards freedom and democracy in the organisation of social and political life. Where is there such a dynamic in the USSR? Nor is it valid to use the historical conditions in which the revolution occurred to justify use of the term socialism for what exists there now—because if we are to be consistent with the Eurocommunist thesis that freedom, democracy and socialism are mutually dependent and we accept that the historical conditions made freedom and democracy impossible, then so too must they have made socialism impossible.

The Eurocommunists have had to borrow their major argument from Trotskyism—that the system of production is socialist but not the political superstructure. This thesis also contradicts the assumption that socialism, freedom and democracy, are interdependent, and what is more, reveals a non-Marxist conception of a socialist system of production. Should not the cornerstone of such a system be the workers' collective appropriation of the means of production? Is it possible to speak of such a collective appropriation if there is no democratic control over every aspect of the socio-political organisation which executes it—in the economy, politics and culture?

Just as there have been various forms of "transition to

capitalism" and various modalities of "capitalism" (from parliamentary democracy to fascist dictatorship), is it not natural that there should also be differing forms of "transition to socialism" and "socialism"? Some of the Eurocommunists have sought to use this analogy—but it is inappropriate. Certainly it is true that the long history of the capitalist mode of production has been characterised by political structures ranging from Bonapartism and Liberalism in the 19th century to formal democracy and fascism in the 20th. But such diversity is explained by the fact that in capitalism the political arena has to be allowed a relative autonomy so that conflicts of interest between different sections of the capitalist class and between that class and the working masses can be mediated and arbitrated to the benefit of the capitalist class as a whole. Authoritarian and exploitative social relations in the sphere of economic production and a separation between the political and the economic areas are both characteristics of capitalism. In the economic sphere there can never be democracy; whether there will be democracy in the political arena or some form of dictatorship will depend on the balance of forces between the classes. In the same way within a formal democracy the degree of democratic rights is always a function of the capacity for struggle of the working class, its level of organisation, class consciousness and unity (accepting that a certain political and ideological pluralism within the class is both necessary and inevitable).

If a substantial degree of democracy were ever introduced into the economy it would signify that the capitalist mode of production was coming to the end of its historical existence. This is the element of truth in the Rome declaration of the PCI and PCF to the effect that the "democratic road to socialism" is a struggle to "take democracy to its logical conclusion". For a socialist mode of production is quite unlike capitalism, in that a purely formal democracy is insufficient and a total lack of democracy makes it quite impossible—what we get instead, as in the USSR, is the appearance of a new ruling class with usufruct of the means of production.

In the transition to a communist mode of production—which would be a long process—democracy would be deepened and extended, reducing the autonomy of the political from the economic. It may be possible, taking into account the varying national and international context and differences of culture and tradition, to envisage differing national paths for the transition to communism. But the acceptance of such national differences should not lead us into the error of lumping together democratic socialism and undemocratic socialism. Although it may be convenient, in these days when regimes as divergent as those of Brezhnev and Ghaddafi call themselves socialist, to use the adjective "democratic", it is strictly speaking redundant. The concept of "undemocratic socialism" is a contradiction in terms.

The conception of the socialist system of production that we have criticised illustrates the continuing presence in Eurocommunist ideology of ideas that originated in the Marxism of the Second International, passed to Lenin and the Third International and became dogmatised by Stalinism: that the abolition of capitalist private property is equivalent to the abolition of capitalist productive relations; that there is a whole gamut of productive forces, in science, technology and the organisation of labour, which are neutral and can just as well serve socialism as capitalism, without the need for any qualitative change; and, based on these two premisses, that everything that alters progress is a function of the level of the productive forces and their material achievement. Only starting from this conception is it possible to assert that there can be a socialist economic base from which the political superstructure has "regressed", a socialist economic infrastructure without a socialist political superstructure.

We can see from this that the question whether or not the Soviet system is socialist not only affects the Eurocommunist parties' relations with Moscow, but their conception of their own socialist transition. We shall return to the second question later. So far as the first is concerned, so long as it retains its present conception Eurocommunism will remain to some extent under Soviet hegemony; the hegemony not just of one of the world's two superpowers, but of a system *which has already realised socialism*. So long as it remains in this situation, Eurocommunism will be unable to develop a strategy capable of linking up with those ever more important social forces and political currents that are struggling for socialism in the East European countries. The question is a key one, because if there is no advance by these forces in the East the cause of socialism in the West could be seriously compromised—just as sixty years ago the frustration of the revolution in the West irremediably mortgaged the victory of the revolution in Russia.

3.

The Democratic Road to Socialism

The Eurocommunist Parties' goal of adapting their conception of socialism and of a strategy of transition to the realities of advanced capitalism has so far taken the concrete form of the so-called "democratic roads to socialism" which each is now seeking to apply in practice within its own national circumstances.

What is meant by this "road"? We shall first consider the official version. Of all the various formulations in documents of the Italian, French and Spanish parties, the most complete and rounded statement is provided in the Rome declaration of the PCI and PCF in November 1975.[37] It can be summarised under the following points:

—Socialism will constitute a higher phase of democracy and freedom: democracy realised in the most complete manner.

—The march towards socialism and the building of a socialist society . . . must be achieved within the framework of a continuous democratisation of economic, social and political life.

—A socialist transformation of society presupposes public control over the principal means of production and exchange, their progressive socialisation, and implementation of democratic economic planning at the national level. The sector of small and medium-sized peasant farms, artisan industry and small and medium-sized industrial and

37. Published by the PCI and PCF 15 November 1975. All emphases are mine—F.C.

commercial enterprises can and must fulfill a specific, positive role in the building of socialism.

—[The parties] declare themselves for . . . the lay nature and democratic functioning of the State . . . Democratic decentralisation of the State must give an increasingly important role to regional and local governments, which must enjoy broad autonomy in the exercise of their powers.

—For the plurality of political parties, for the right to existence and activity of opposition parties, for the free formation of majorities and minorities and the possibility of their alternating democratically.

—For the freedom of activity and autonomy of the trade unions.

—[The parties] attribute essential importance to the development of democracy in the workplace, allowing the workers to participate in the running of their firms, with real rights and extensive decision-making powers.

—Guarantee and development of all freedoms which are a product both of the great bourgeois-democratic revolutions and of the great popular struggles of this century, headed by the working class. [This is followed by the enumeration of these freedoms.]

—This [socialist] transformation can only be the result of great, powerful struggles and broad mass movements, uniting the majority of the people around the working class. It requires the existence, guarantee and development of democratic institutions fully representative of popular sovereignty and the free exercise of direct, proportional universal suffrage. It is in this framework that the two parties—which have always respected and will always respect the verdict of universal suffrage—conceive the rise of the working people to the leadership of the State.

—[The two parties] attach a value of principle to all these conditions of democratic life. Their position is not tactical, but derived from their analysis of the specific objective and historical conditions of their countries and from their reflection on international experiences as a whole.

These positions of principle summarise the essential content of numerous programmatic and strategic statements of the PCI, PCF and PCE[38] in which they have broadly set out their views on:

—the structural economic, social and political reforms that would characterise a process of transition to socialism;
—the new power bloc, constructed by means of a system of social and political alliances around the working class, that would be capable of carrying through these reforms;
—the forms of struggle by which this new bloc would come to power and retain it;
—an international policy for the process of transition.

But before we proceed to these more concrete questions, it seems sensible to tackle the issue of principle that informs the whole notion of the "democratic road" as set out above—the concept of the relationship between democracy and socialism according to which neither is capable of being fully realised without the other. This problem could be approached from various angles, but I shall restrict myself here to those two that seem to me now most fruitful methodologically; (1) the vicissitudes of this relationship—the different ways in which it has been understood and practiced—in the history of Marxism and of the Marxist movement; (2) the ways in which it is at variance with the economic and political structures characteristic of advanced capitalism.

The Historical Experience

From the outset of their experience of revolutionary struggle and of their development of historical materialism, Marx and

38. Berlinguer first proposed his "historic compromise" in a series of articles he wrote after the defeat in Chile. The line was confirmed at the 14th Congress of the PCI and further developed in subsequent proceedings of the Central Committee. In the case of the PCF, the evolution can be traced from the 1971 party programme which was used as the basis for negotiating the Common Programme of the Union of the Left, through the Rome Declaration, to the 22nd Congress. The 8th Congress of the PCE in 1973 adopted the first draft of the Manifesto and Programme and the final text was approved in September 1975 at a national conference.

Engels postulated a conception of democracy which implied a basic contradiction between democracy and bourgeois rule. Writing late in 1845 while he was working with Marx on *The German Ideology*, Engels claimed that "Democracy has become a mass, a proletarian principle. The masses do not always clearly grasp this meaning of democracy, which is the only accurate one, but everybody includes in the notion of democracy, however confusedly, the aspiration to social justice". "Communism is the democracy for our time." In another text written shortly before the *Communist Manifesto* he advanced the thesis that "the political rule of the proletariat is in all the civilised lands a *necessary* consequence of democracy", thus formulating as an objective tendency what Marx was to put programmatically in the *Manifesto*: "the first step in the revolution by the working class is to raise the proletariat to the position of ruling class, to win the battle of democracy."[39]

The premise of an objective contradiction between democracy and bourgeois rule and inversely of an objective correspondence between democracy and proletarian rule was a key element in Marx's and Engels's theory of revolution on the eve of 1848, and was confirmed by their practical experience of the revolutionary process. After the defeat of the revolution Marx described the republican constitution adopted by the French Constituent Assembly under pressure of the revolutionary movement as constraining the rule of the bourgeoisie within the bounds of "democratic conditions which constantly help its enemies towards victory and endanger the very basis of bourgeois society."[40]

Against this risk, even before the Constitution was completed or promulgated, the French republican bourgeoisie used the army to crush the main bastion of democracy, the Paris proletariat. Confronted with a similar danger, the German liberal bourgeoisie made a pact with the absolutist monarchy and called in Tsarist armies to its assistance. Marx

39. For a longer discussion of this theme, see my book *Marx, Engels y La Revolución de 1848*, Madrid 1975, pp. 39–40.
40. Karl Marx, *Surveys from Exile*, NLR/Penguin, London 1973, p. 71.

concluded from these defeats (to be succeeded by so many others down to our own time) not that the struggle for democracy was futile, but rather that it was subversive—demonstrating in deeds the anti-democratic nature of the bourgeoisie and the anti-bourgeois nature of democracy. But he also drew the lesson that when the revolution is faced with the need for an armed struggle, universal suffrage must be backed up by an armed strength greater than that of the bourgeoisie. To "win the battle of democracy", the first step in the proletarian revolution, it was necessary to destroy the State apparatus which the previous ruling class had created to secure its rule and to insulate it from any democratic process. In order to take this first step the proletariat should make alliances with the peasantry and the urban petty-bourgeoisie, whose interests are also at odds with bourgeois rule, albeit the contradiction was of a different order to that between the proletariat and the bourgeoisie.

For Marx and Engels democracy was the political system suited to all these sectors and classes which the *Manifesto* saw as an "immense majority" gathered under the hegemony of the proletariat, "the only truly revolutionary class". In their analysis and in their political practice at that period the struggle for democracy stands out as the political expression *par excellence* of the proletarian revolution. So it was to remain throughout their life and work. Not just for countries (such as Germany at that time) where the revolution would initially include some anti-feudal tasks, but also for those such as England where capitalism was fully established. Indeed Chartism provided the first historical example of a "democratic road to socialism" and had a considerable influence on the political strategy of Marx and Engels.[41]

The formula of "the dictatorship of the proletariat" which at first sight contradicts the privileged role assigned by Marx to democracy was not his own invention. It derives from the most radical social current of Jacobinism, which was mainly

41. *Marx, Engels y La Revolución de 1848*, pp. 13–14.

represented in the 1848 revolution by Blanqui's party. It was from them that Marx borrowed the term in 1850, giving it a substantially altered sense. He used the term only rarely.[42] Many Marxist commentators, including Lenin, have shown that for Marx it meant "proletarian class rule" and implied a very broad democracy for the immense majority. Engels polemicised against those who saw in the notion a negation of democracy, using the Paris Commune as a concrete example of dictatorship of the proletariat. In any case, for Marx the use of the term "dictatorship" in the formula "dictatorship of the proletariat" or "dictatorship of the bourgeoisie" never held the meaning which it has universally acquired in practical politics since the Stalinist and Fascist dictatorships. That is more than sufficient reason to correct a formula rendered so ambiguous by historical experience.

The whole history of capitalist social formations confirms the contradiction between democracy and bourgeois rule. Every aspect of democracy in the structure of State and civil society has been won by the struggles of the working class and other sections of the masses, although sometimes fractions of the bourgeoisie have led the masses, mobilising them for their own ends against other fractions of the bourgeoisie or the feudal aristocracy. The fact that the bourgeoisie is sometimes obliged to adapt the form of its power to these democratic conquests, to "recuperate" them by the use of its multiple weapons of coercion and ideology in order to reestablish its control on a new basis, does not signify the disappearance of the contradiction. It has then simply shifted onto new terrain, assuming a new form.

Of particular interest in this respect is the work which Engels produced towards the end of his life and of the century, in 1895. Reflecting on the balance sheet of fifty years of struggle for socialism since the revolutions of 1848, he picked out two factors that had transformed the conditions of class struggle in the Western capitalist countries—the growth of political democracy (a product of the rising strength of the proletariat) and changes in the military apparatus of the

42. ibid, p. 312.

capitalist states.[43] Engels considered that improved military technology and the increased size of armies condemned to failure "the old style of rebellion with street barricades". He did not reject the possibility of future armed struggles, but they would have to be of a different type. His fundamental conclusion was that "the epoch of surprise attacks, of revolutions led by small conscious minorities at the head of unconscious masses is past. Where it is a question of completely transforming the organisation of society, the masses must intervene directly, they must understand for themselves what is at stake and for what they are to give their blood and their lives." That would demand "long and persistent labour". Engels counterposed to "the old style of rebellion" what he called "the *effective* use of universal suffrage" practised by the German Social-Democratic party, which had managed in a few years to win more than a quarter of votes cast in the Reichstag elections. It was obvious in the light of this experience, according to Engels, "that the State institutions through which the bourgeoisie organises its domination offer the working class new opportunities to struggle against those very institutions . . . The universal irony of history stands everything on its head. We the 'revolutionaries', the 'subversive elements' do much better with legal methods than with the methods of illegality and subversion. The parties of order, as they call themselves, find themselves trapped by the very legality they have created". In the document known as his Testament, Engels outlined this prospect: "We can now reckon with the support of $2\frac{1}{4}$ million voters. If this advance continues we shall by the end of this century have won a majority of the intermediate layers of society, petty-bourgeois and small peasants, and shall be a decisive power in the land before which every other power must bow, whether they will or no. To maintain this uninterrupted progress until it overwhelms the present system of government; not to waste our shock force, which grows daily stronger, in skirmishes, but to conserve it until the decisive day—that is our principal task."

43. See Engels, 'Introduction to *The Class Struggle in France*,' in Marx-Engels, *Selected Works*, London 1970, p. 654.

These strategic and tactical prescriptions of Engels could be read in different ways. For Rosa Luxemburg they indicated a policy of building up forces ready for the day when the inevitable catastrophic crisis of capitalism would place "the final battle" on the agenda. Bernstein and the other openly reformist leaders interpreted Engels in their own legalist, electoralist, gradualist and pacifist way. Kautsky and the "orthodox centre" criticised Bernstein's version but acted as if they agreed with him. The rapid and imposing electoral successes of German Social-Democracy (the first to be won by any party of Marxist inspiration) exercised a sort of fascination over the principal leaders of the mass of militants in the party, which even Engels did not entirely escape, as his "Testament" indicates. The document was used as an authoritative justification for the electoralist line that led to the capitulation of the SPD in 1914. For that reason Rosa Luxemburg partially revised her earlier opinion to criticise it in 1918, in the midst of the German Revolution; but some of her criticisms of the Bolsheviks at the same period show that she still shared the central idea in those last thoughts of Engels—that only the conscious action of the great majority could accomplish the socialist revolution, which necessarily implied democracy.

The experience of Social-Democracy in Germany and other countries both before and after the First World War provides a historical illustration of the dangers that lie in wait along the "democratic road to socialism" once the basic contradiction between democracy and bourgeois rule is forgotten—and with it the inevitable consequence that at some stage, whether before or after the advance of democracy has brought the workers to power, the bourgeoisie will use every means available to it to prevent the completion of the process.

After the First World War German Social-Democracy made spectacular progress electorally, only to be cut short brutally by Nazism—to which it capitulated without a fight, just as it had to the imperialist war. The same fate overtook Austrian Social-Democracy, the party furthest to the left within the Second International—though its revolutionary honour was salvaged by resistance of its workers' militias in the bloody days of February 1934. In the elections of April 1927 the ÖSPD had won 43% of the vote over the whole country and a substantial majority in Vienna. Otto Bauer, its main leader, wrote a triumphal article that recalls the optimistic prospect that Engels had outlined for German Social-Democracy in 1895: "In 1920 we had 36% of the vote. In the last elections nearly 40%. Now we have almost 43%. In six and a half years we have increased our strength by approximately 7%. What more do we need? To reach power we must travel about the same distance again that we have come since 1920 . . . Another one or two elections and we shall have put an end to bourgeois governments."[44] But at the end of that time it was the bourgeois government that put an end to Social-Democracy.

The original sin of Social-Democracy, which soon became its second nature, was its restriction of democracy within limits compatible with the rule of the bourgeoisie, in every given conjuncture. To give ideological cover and justification to this adaptation, it attributed a democratic vocation to the bourgeoisie which the latter proceeded to deny whenever the progress of democracy put the capitalist system in any real danger. Bourgeois denial of democracy is nowhere so patent as in the basic structures of society, its relations of production. The reason is simple—no individual capitalist or capitalist institution could submit to democratic control by the workers that they exploit. It is not a matter of will, but of the very nature of the capitalist system; and the same holds true in varying degree for all the other organs that underpin or reproduce the system—the army, the police, the courts, education, or ideological apparatuses.

From a Marxist standpoint Social-Democracy should be condemned not for its excess of democratic zeal, but for keeping it within the bounds prescribed by the bourgeoisie. There was another aspect to this original sin too: an economist interpretation of the basic contradiction of capitalism—the

44. See my introduction to the Spanish edition of Ernst Fischer's Memoirs, *Recuerdos y Reflexiones*, Madrid 1976, p. 4.

conservation of capitalist relations of production and the growing socialisation of the forces of production. In this interpretation, the contradiction generated an objective tendency which would inevitably lead to the gradual transformation of capitalism into socialism. The prospect for socialism, flanked on one side by an economic determinism and on the other by a democratic determinism, seemed assured without any need for a revolutionary rupture. The task of Social-Democracy was simply to assist the process by promoting whatever reforms were permitted at any particular time by the limits of democracy. The centrist tendency around Kautsky made formal criticisms of this concept and retained the idea of a "qualitative leap", of "revolution", but in practice as we have said differed little from the reformist Right.

As for the Left, in place of the Right's fatalistic gradualism, it offered a fatalistic catastrophism, likewise rooted in economism. The basic contradiction of capitalism would lead inevitably to a "final crisis", that would constitute the objective premiss of a revolution. By parliamentary and trade union action but also by the use of other forms of mass action such as the political strike the revolutionary forces could help to bring about this crisis. This Left problematic was developed mainly in the aftermath of the 1905 Russian revolution.

A long period of relatively peaceful and prosperous development of Western capitalism, due in large part to colonial exploitation, had reduced Marxism to a mechanical theory of a gradual transformation of capitalism into socialism, and a reformist political strategy that corresponded to it. Both were brutally put in question by the first great crisis to overtake capitalism in its imperialist phase. Revolution seemed once more to be on the agenda in 1917–21. But the great majority of the workers' movement in the West, educated in the ideology and practice of Social-Democracy, was in no condition to take advantage of the crisis. Only in Russia did the revolution triumph as a social revolution. In all other countries (Hungary, Bavaria, Finland, Italy, Spain) the defeat of attempted proletarian revolutions cleared the path for dictatorships of a fascist, military or clerical variety.

Even in Germany—the Bolsheviks' best hope—the newly formed Communist Party's efforts of 1919 and 1923 met no success. The right-wing Social-Democratic leaders, now government ministers, did not hesitate to repress the Berlin rising of workers and Spartacists (Communists), in the course of which Rosa Luxemburg and Karl Liebknecht were assassinated. Under Social-Democratic hegemony, the German Revolution stopped short with the overthrow of the monarchy and the installation of the new republic. The majority of the working class, however, saw in this limited result a great victory—it seemed to them that within the republican framework the peaceful, parliamentary, gradualist road to socialism was even more assured. The imperialist war had been nothing but a bloody interlude in this steady progress. According to Kautsky's theory of "ultra-imperialism" the objective development of imperialism led inexorably to capitalist concentration on a world scale, transcending the inter-state and international contradictions of capitalism and creating the ideal conditions for its transformation into socialism. Kautsky glossed over the fact that a transcendence of these contradictions within the framework of imperialism presupposed new catastrophic wars and great class defeats for the proletariat and its allies, and victories for capital.

Only one proletarian and socialist revolution—so defined by the vanguard which led it—triumphed: the Russian revolution. The Bolsheviks soon discovered that their main enemy—without whose help the Tsarist counter-revolution would have held little danger—was the international "democratic bourgeoisie". France, England and the USA, victorious in the imperialist war, immediately established a *cordon sanitaire* and sent their troops to assist the White Guards. The revolution found itself deprived of what Lenin and the Bolshevik party had always considered to be the minimum condition, the *sine qua non* for their revolution to be consolidated as a *socialist* revolution—the German *socialist* revolution. The Social-Democrats of the victorious "bourgeois democracies" were prepared to defend the Russian Revolution, but would not lift a finger to advance that "world revolution" which Lenin believed was ripe. Worse yet, Social-Democratic theorists and political leaders considered that in a country like Russia any attempt to push the revolution beyond its initial anti-tsarist, bourgeois-democratic stage was an adventure that was bound to fail, and would harm both the Russian and the international workers' movement.

From the outset, therefore, the "bourgeois democracies" and social-democracy were implacably opposed to the October Revolution and its world party, the Communist International. This was to have a profound effect on Communist theoretical positions and practical attitude towards democracy.

We seldom find the concept "proletarian democracy" in Lenin's work prior to the revolution. The term "democracy" is often used with no qualification, usually connoting bourgeois. Lenin often, as was general in the Second International, used expressions that implied the acknowledgment of a democratic tendency in the bourgeoisie.[45] But he also frequently emphasised and warned against the unreliability of this bourgeois democratism. On the eve of the Russian Revolution, pointing to the antagonism between imperialist capitalism and democracy, he described imperialism as the negation of democracy. He also criticised other Bolsheviks for underestimating the role of democracy in the anti-capitalist struggle. "Socialism is impossible without democracy because: (1) the proletariat cannot perform the socialist revolution unless it prepares for it by the struggle for democracy; (2) victorious socialism cannot consolidate its victory and bring humanity to the withering away of the State without implementing full democracy."[46]

In *State and Revolution* (1917) we find the first theorisation

45. See for example in Lenin, "Reply to P. Kievski" (I. Piatakov) in his *Collected Works*, Vol. 23, pp. 25, 27: "Capitalism engenders democratic aspirations in the masses, creates democratic institutions..."; "the democratic institutions created and distorted by the bourgeoisie".

46. Lenin, "A Caricature of Marxism", *Collected Works*, Vol. 23, p. 74.

of an idea which Lenin had not advanced at the time of the 1905 revolution or subsequently—that a Soviet form of state is best suited for the transition to socialism. He still, however, did not counterpose this form to those of representative democracy. The Bolshevik party was for the Constituent Assembly and only opted for its dissolution when it found itself in a minority within it. At that stage it appeared to favour incorporating all past democratic gains without exception into Soviet democracy. But after the famous dissolution of the Constituent Assembly, a marked shift occurred which was undoubtedly determined by the factors we have already mentioned—the internal opposition of non-Bolshevik socialist currents, the hostile attitude of international social-democracy and the intervention by the "bourgeois democratic" states.

In his theses on "bourgeois democracy and the dictatorship of the proletariat" addressed to the First Congress of the Communist International, Lenin caricatured the limitations of democracy under bourgeois governments to the point where the conquest of democratic rights by workers under capitalism appears effectively negligible. Freedom of assembly was now described as "a hollow phrase even in the most democratic of bourgeois republics"; freedom of the press was "a deception"; real opportunity to enjoy democratic rights and freedoms "has never existed, even approximately, in the best and the most democratic bourgeois republics." Moreover Lenin attacked "those theorists who defend democracy without seeing its *bourgeois character*".[47] Curiously enough Lenin's acceptance of the bourgeois nature of democracy put him in the same company with social-democracy. The latter used it to justify reformist concepts; Lenin used it to reduce all democratic rights and freedoms to the level of "tricks" and "empty phrases". This same tendency shows in his polemic against Kautsky and other works, and in the documents of the Comintern, so long as the leader of the Russian Revolution and the International continued to

47. Lenin, "Thesis and Report on Bourgeois Democracy and the Dictatorship of the Proletariat", *Collected Works*, Vol. 28, pp. 460–1, 465, 467.

believe in the advance of the "world revolution" and the need to combat the West European proletariat's "illusions in bourgeois democracy". To the latter he now counterposed "proletarian democracy", the only "true" democracy whose perfect, finished form had been discovered in the system of councils or *soviets*.

In Comintern ideology there now developed an essential conflict between council democracy and representative or delegated democracy. Only the first was suited to proletarian rule; the second was designed exclusively for bourgeois rule.

Before long, however, it was obvious that the only concrete material example of a State and social organisation which had grown out of such councils—the Soviet system that developed out of the February and October revolutions—differed radically from the theoretical model of this form of democracy (as outlined in Lenin's *State and Revolution* and in the works of Gramsci, Pannekoek and others). Nor were these divergences minor variations, the kind of inevitable specificities that will supervene between any socio-political reality and its theoretical representation; they were contradictions that put the essence of the model itself in question. The effective workers' democracy of the model was short-circuited by the reality of a system of military, police, economic, administrative, juridical and ideological apparatuses which had escaped all popular control and were now the real power centres—in turn organised and controlled by the central apparatus of the single party. The structure of the Soviets progressively lost its democratic content, as it was converted into a transmission belt (like the trade-unions or other mass organisations) of the party and state apparatuses (while the latter in turn functioned as transmission belts of the party apparatus). The progressive liquidation of inner-party democracy increased the anti-democratic character of the whole system. "Proletarian democracy" then came to exclude the proletariat, not to speak of every other section of the working masses. After the death of Lenin, during the epoch of Stalin, all these processes were intensified, until the "Soviet" regime was transformed into an implacable dictatorship over the toiling masses. The process which thus began so clearly in the period of the Civil War cannot be said to have led inevitably to Stalinism, but it must have been a major factor in that phenomenon.

There can be no doubt of the significance of the frustrated proletarian revolutions in the West, the isolation of the Russian revolution that followed and the intervention of the capitalist powers. But there were other factors inherent in the nature of the revolution that weighed heavily in the process. The first of these was the fact that while as an anti-feudal, anti-tsarist upheaval, the Russian Revolution had enjoyed the support of an immense majority of the population, only a tiny minority (which enjoyed conjunctural support at first from the mass of the peasantry) wanted a *socialist* revolution. Hence any democratic form of constitution posed problems.

To get round the difficulty and ensure that what remained of soviet democracy should only develop in the direction desired, the working class was over-represented by comparison with the peasantry, large sections of the petty-bourgeoisie received no representation at all, those socialist or democratic currents which were opposed for political or ideological reasons to the Bolsheviks were suppressed, and all power was concentrated into the apparatus. A mechanism was thereby set in motion which would eventually destroy all trace of democracy.

Two features facilitated the process. The first was the complete lack of democratic tradition in Russian society. The people had struggled against the Tsarist autocracy in the name of democracy, but apart from the brief interlude between the February Revolution and the first moves against soviet democracy, they had never experienced it. The second lay in the nature of the vanguard which directed the revolution from October onwards. Lenin's theory made the party the custodian of Marxist theory, depositary and guarantee of the historic interests of the proletariat into which its task was to instil a socialist consciousness. The party was not subject to any democratic judgment that the masses might pass on it, but set its own course. It was ideologically prepared, therefore, should the masses fail to reach the level of consciousness required by "historic necessity", to accept a position of authority, of guardianship, over them. In a word, should the free expression of "proletarian democracy" run counter to what the party considered to be in the interests of the revolution, the party was ideologically predisposed to substitute for that free expression.

With this ideological training, foreign to the Marxism of Marx, the Bolshevik party proceeded—with the best will in the world—to make a virtue of necessity: the restriction and suppression of democracy, first justified by an emergency situation, became the realisation of a "higher form of democracy". But whereas the enlightened despotism of absolute monarchs had on occasion contributed to the enlightenment of bourgeois society, the enlightened despotism of the Communist Party has cast no light but rather a dark shadow on socialist society. The ideas contained in Engels' "will" and in Lenin's dictum before the revolution that socialism could not be achieved without the fullest democracy, have been amply confirmed by the experience of the Russian Revolution and of the other revolutions that have tried to follow the same path.

The criticisms and warnings which Rosa Luxemburg addressed to Russian leadership in 1918—at the same time as she emphasised the responsibility of the German proletariat for its failure to make its own revolution and rendered homage to the audacity of the Bolsheviks—proved to be prophetic. She condemned their "cold disdain for the constituent assembly, universal suffrage, freedom of the press and of assembly, in short the whole gamut of basic democratic rights of the mass of the people." "It is a notorious but incontestable fact that popular rule by the masses is quite inconceivable without unrestricted freedom of the press, free association and free assembly." "In place of the representative bodies based on general elections of the whole people, Lenin and Trotsky have set the soviets up to be the only authentic representative organ of the working masses. But with the political life of the whole country suffocated even the soviets will be unable to escape a creeping paralysis. Without general elections, unrestricted freedom of the press and of assembly and the free clash of opinion, the life will go out of every political institution leaving nothing but a dead facade; the only reality will be the bureaucracy."[48]

When it became clear that the revolutionary wave had receded in Europe, Lenin was soon confronted within the Comintern by a leftist nihilism towards parliamentary and other forms of "bourgeois democracy" for which he was himself partly responsible. In *Left-Wing Communism, an Infantile Disorder* and other writings and speeches of the period, Lenin insisted on the need to use these institutions for propaganda purposes and to forge links with the masses. But when the time was ripe the task of the revolution would not be to transform them or dialectically to draw out their democratic content—they were to be swept away. They were seen as mere "creations of capitalism" or of the "bourgeoisie", instead of achievements of mass working class struggle within a given balance of forces, and as such organs in which there is always a latent or manifest conflict between an authoritarian, bureaucratic formalism which is the marks of bourgeois pressure on them and their democratic content.

In the new conjuncture Lenin and the Comintern advocated a policy of United Front in which the communists were to "make use of bourgeois democracy" to fight for economic and political demands and to resist fascism—newly installed in Italy and a threat in other countries. The United Front was conceived as a strategy that would allow the Communists to accumulate forces while they waited for a favourable conjuncture from which to launch the direct struggle for the dictatorship of the proletariat that would destroy bourgeois democracy and install a "soviet" democracy after the Russian model. While accepting the possibility of "workers' governments" or "governments of workers and peasants" with a common front between socialists and communists, the Com-

48. See Rosa Luxemburg, "The Russian Revolution", in M.-A. Waters (ed). *Rosa Luxemburg Speaks*, New York 1970, pp. 379, 389, 391. "A freedom that is reserved only for the supporters of the government, only for the members of the party, however numerous these might be, is not freedom. Freedom is only ever freedom for those who think differently." (p. 389).

intern still insisted that "only a workers' government, composed of Communists can realise the complete dictatorship of the proletariat."[49] In the most sectarian period of Comintern, from the Sixth Congress in 1928 to the turn of 1934, any attempt to take tactical advantage from the contradictions that existed between "bourgeois democracy" and social-democrats on the one hand and the fascists and other reactionary forces was abandoned. Already in 1924, with Lenin scarcely dead, Stalin had advanced the thesis that "social-democracy is objectively the moderate wing of fascism".[50] Later it would be classified as "social fascism". In 1931 the Comintern decided that to draw any distinction between "bourgeois democracy" and fascism was a "liberal concept" since "fascism is *organically* derived from bourgeois democracy".[51] Here the concept of democracy as an essentially bourgeois political form ideally suited to capitalist class domination had been taken to its ultimate ideological conclusion; applied in the policies of the Comintern's "national sections" with disastrous effects, it was largely responsible for Hitler's rout of the German party.

The defeat in Germany and the threat of Nazi aggression against the Soviet Union subsequently produced a spectacular turn by the Comintern; the central objective of the International was now declared to be the defence of democracy—and in those countries where the battle had already been lost, its reconquest. But this democracy was still no more than a stage during which forces might be accumulated so that when a favourable conjuncture occurred the dictatorship of the proletariat could be installed according to the Soviet model: this at a time when the transformation of that model into a police state was being given the finishing touches by the trials of the revolutionary old guard and the deportation of millions of communists and non-party workers to concentration

49. *Manifestes, Theses et Resolutions des Guatre Premiers Congrès Mondiaux de l'Internationale Communiste*, Milan, Feltrinelli 1967, p. 159.

50. Stalin, "The International Situation" (in September 1924) in *Works*, Vol. 6, Moscow 1953.

51. See the sections on *The Revolution Frustrated (France)* and *The Revolution Frustrated (Italy)* in the second part of *The Communist Movement* (op. cit.).

camps. Of course this repression was systematically concealed from the outside world, and the bulk of the Soviet people were equally ignorant, at least of the scale and the methods employed.

The authorities took the same care in keeping the repressive operations secret as in carrying them out. The few cases that did receive publicity, either by accident or by deliberate intention of the regime, were justified as the defence of the revolution against traitors, saboteurs or secret agents of capitalism. We have already referred in the second part of this essay to the blind faith in the "socialist homeland" which most Communists professed at that time and which led them to place complete trust in the official version of events. But even in the socialist parties and other democratic organisations within the capitalist countries, many only half believed the denunciation made by Trotsky and other Russian revolutionaries—while they naturally believed the allegations of reactionary ideologues and politicians even less. The counterpart of the dense screen of secrecy with which the Party-State concealed its oppression was the shining facade of the 1936 (Stalin) Constitution, according to the official propaganda "the most democratic in the world". It proclaimed as reality everything that the very structure and methods of the regime denied. In addition to the difficulty of looking lucidly into the Soviet system, Western socialists and democrats were by now quite rightly more concerned about the fascist threat.

The new policy of the Popular Front, extending to liberal fractions of the bourgeoisie or petty-bourgeoisie, was made necessary by the threat of fascism and made possible by the turn of Comintern policy. The Soviet Union made alliances with those "democratic" capitalist states whose interests were opposed to the expansionist aims of the fascist states. Later the formation of the "grand alliance" between the USSR, the USA and Britain allowed—indeed demanded—the expansion of the Popular Fronts into national anti-fascist alliances which included every element from the Communists through to major sections of the bourgeoisie. The dose of democracy that was included in these "democratic platforms" depended on the national and international balance of forces in each case. As we noted earlier, it was in this context that the CPs made their first efforts to work out democratic "national roads to socialism". For ten years (from 1935 and the Sixth Congress of the Communist International to 1947 and the first year of the Cold War, not counting the two years of the German-Soviet pact) the question of democracy was at the centre of every Communist party's strategy.

The parties that played the main role in developing and applying the new line were either those (notably the Italian and Spanish parties) that had lived through the experience of a fascist dictatorship or of a struggle to prevent the installation of one, or else parties like those of France or Czechoslovakia that had grown up in countries with well-established democratic traditions. Dimitrov and Togliatti were the main theoretical figures. Togliatti in particular brought new analytical elements to bear on the problem of socialist revolution in the West, and his contribution was to have the greatest and most lasting impact of any thinker on the West European Communist movement until the "discovery" of Gramsci (which in Italy began in 1947 with the publication of the *Prison Notebooks*, but did not occur outside Italy until the 1960s).

The Italian Communist Party had been the first that had to confront the problems of fighting for democracy against a fascist dictatorship. Although Gramsci's concept of that fight was entirely framed within the Leninist strategic schema, he enriched it with his analysis of Italy's peculiar social structure in which the problem of the alliance between workers and peasantry took the specific form of the "Vatican question" and the "question of the South". His connection with the Italian party was loosened by his imprisonment in 1926 and his differences with the leadership of the Soviet party—and therefore also with the Comintern. The leadership passed to Togliatti who adapted to the ultrasectarian policies of the Comintern between 1928–34 and ensured that Gramsci's criticisms were not made known or discussed within the party.

From 1934 onwards Togliatti readopted the Gramscian analysis, modified by gradualism and tacticism characteristic of his own vision. Drawing on the experience of democracy in the Spanish Republic during the Civil War, he formulated the notion of a "new democracy" in which the working-class, while keeping within the limits of capitalism and conserving all the democratic institutions and freedoms that had been won under capitalism, would win a hegemonic position and carry through social and economic reforms tending to go beyond the system. The idea reappeared after the defeat of fascism in the Second World War in those countries of Eastern Europe that had been liberated by the Soviet army. But in practice it was the army of liberation that took over the dominant role in these "new democracies" (or "popular democracies" as they later became known); under their protection all decisive centres of power, especially the army and police, were captured by the Communist Party, other parties were given minor "walk-on" parts and any autonomous action by the population and the working class was kept strictly within the limits determined by the Communist leadership.

With the onset of the Cold War Moscow ordered the foreclosure of what democracy remained in these "popular democracies" and the Soviet model was adopted with only minor variations. Bucharest, Budapest, Prague and Warsaw all had their own "Moscow trials". Any Communist leader or cadre who offered any resistance to the "Russification" of their party—or was thought likely to—was imprisoned or executed. The crime of which they were accused was "Titoism"— because Tito then personified the first successful resistance to Moscow's control within the Communist movement.

In Western Europe the strategy of "new democracy" developed by those communists, left socialists and other radical democrats who had formed the nucleus of the Resistance had started to put in question the structure of capitalism. Then, in the famous *svolta di Salerno*, Togliatti persuaded the Italian party—with the agreement of Moscow—to accept that the Resistance should make a last-minute compromise with the monarchy and the bedraggled forces of fascism. In France too the PCF compromised with de Gaulle's *France Libre*, with the approval of Moscow. Therewith the advanced democratic platforms of the various resistance movements faded away. The Communist Parties, once the major political and military force of the Resistance, increasingly yielded to the demands of the bourgeois parties in the governments of antifascist national unity which were formed in 1945, with the American Army behind them.

It is not our purpose here to discuss the vexed questions of whether any other policy was possible for the French and Italian parties—not a direct struggle for power, but at least an *offensive* fight for the major changes proposed by the Resistance. What is clear is that neither party ever even explored the possibility, because they chose to subordinate their policy to the decisions of the "Grand Alliance", and to respect the share-out of zones of influence by the "Big Powers" at Yalta. The PCI platform for the 1946 Constituent Assembly elections stated quite categorically that "the great democratic powers have the task of guiding the reorganisation of the entire world to secure peace and justice for all. Italy must seek its salvation in the unity of these great powers".[52] Never before had the illusion been so strong within the CPs that a *major sector* of the bourgeoisie was going to submit loyally to the rules of the democratic game and accept that the workers should play an ever more important role in every sphere of society and the State until a new order emerged from them.

To emphasise the gradual nature that any "new democracy" would assume in the advanced countries of the capitalist West, Togliatti started to use instead the term "progressive democracy". The contribution of the Italian and French CPs in government was decisive in maintaining order and restoring capitalist production, ensuring that it was not disrupted by the impetuous resurgence of the workers movement. When they were expelled from office in the countries of Western Europe in 1947, it was more for reasons of foreign policy, than because of the needs of the bourgeoisie in internal

52. Togliatti, *El Partido Comunista Italiano*, Barcelona 1976, p. 116.

affairs—a foreign policy now totally dependent on American imperialism. For the USA had decided to make the most of the military advantage it possessed in the atom bomb and of the economic advantage it possessed because of the fact that the war had seriously weakened the Soviet economy yet greatly strengthened the American economy. It therefore decided to go onto the offensive against its recent "great ally" of the war against Hitler, to try to improve on its portion of the Yalta shareout. For the Communist Parties—who still regarded the USSR as the country where socialism had first been built and from which it would be exported to other areas—the "defence of the Soviet Union" was still the first principle of their policy, so they were clearly incompatible with the new American strategy and were eliminated from government.

In fact, as I have argued elsewhere, the "Cold War" was no more than a sparring match between two superpowers who had decided that the real balance of forces had changed since Yalta and now sought to change the division of the world accordingly. Each was determined that the conflict should not escalate to the level of a direct confrontation which could prove disastrous for both. In Asia the struggle to establish a new balance of forces found its critical arena in Korea, in Europe in Germany.

The Cold War revealed once more just how tightly Moscow continued to control the Communist Parties. To counter American imperialism's intervention in West Europe and other regions of the world, Moscow developed its own imperialist policy towards the countries of its own sphere of influence (its aims and methods showed some similarities and some differences from those of Washington). Moscow received unconditional support, with no word of criticism, from the CPs.

Another effect of the Cold War was that any exploration of a "national road" to socialism which Moscow decided might obstruct its regroupment of forces against its American rival or might put in question the Soviet model of socialism must be stopped (this was the threat of "Titoism"). In reality even if the "national roads" of this period, 1945–47, contained the seed of this threat, they did not imply a rejection of the Soviet model. Rather—as with the policy of the Popular Front, of which they were simply a repetition on a broader scale—they were conceived as a new route to arrive at it. They still assumed the Soviet regime to be the highest form of socialist democracy, which required the undisputed leadership of the Communist Parties. The Cold War thus revealed the existence of a "double bottomed" strategy in the thought of the Western Communist Parties.

When there was a revival of the "national roads" after 1956, that too—like their burial in 1947—was the direct result of a turn in the domestic and foreign policy of the USSR. The Cold War had reached stalemate when an internal crisis developed with the death of Stalin. The majority fraction of the leadership of the CPSU decided that the best way to keep the system together would be a policy of "destalinisation" or what they described as "the development of socialist democracy". Soviet foreign policy was now directed towards a far-reaching understanding with the USA.

The CPSU also at this time raised the possibility that in the "bourgeois democracies" of the capitalist world the working class might come to power by "peaceful parliamentary means" under Communist leadership. The motives for this Soviet initiative were complex. In part it was an acknowledgment of the preference that the Western parties had shown for a national democratic road prior to 1947; they would clearly find subordination to the Soviet centre more acceptable on that basis. At the same time it kept them within the limits of ideological orthodoxy and the political needs of Moscow's new internal policy and attuned their strategic orientation more to the new Russian foreign policy.

The CPSU was ready now to concede the possibility of a "peaceful parliamentary road" to socialism in the West, because the fact that both superpowers now possessed the capacity to annihilate each other seemed to exclude the prospect of another world war. This left room for peaceful co-existence and competition between the two systems—capitalist and socialist. Since (according to Soviet analysis) capitalism was struggling in its "general crisis" and so was incapable of any further development of its productive forces, whereas the socialist system was going forward triumphantly from one five-year plan to the next, the moment would eventually arrive when the balance of forces on the world scale tipped decisively in favour of the socialist system. (At its 22nd Congress in 1961 the CPSU solemnly announced that the Soviet Union—which was now on the way to communism—would have overtaken the USA in every field by the close of the 1970s.) Once that stage was reached, if the Communists and their allies were to win a majority in parliament no one would be in a position to prevent them from taking power peacefully.

The 1957 conference in Moscow therefore fixed "the struggle for peace" as the number one task for the Communist Parties of the capitalist countries.[53] To ensure the peaceful evolution of the two systems was to secure the (peaceful) victory of the socialist revolution in those countries. If they were to be ready to take advantage of the moment when this decisive shift in the balance of forces occurred, and help to bring it about, the Communist Parties would have to make use of every institution and method of "bourgeois democracy" in the "struggle for peace", which necessitated an even broader system of alliances than had the Popular Fronts. Naturally before the transition to socialism could be completed there would have to be a "dictatorship of the proletariat". Providing always that the one essential "general law" for the transition was fulfilled—the Communist Party in command—the dictatorship might take different forms. There was the "highest" or Soviet form, or the form adopted by the "popular democracies" with fictitious non-communist parties (manipulated by the real CP), fictitious parliaments and fictitious freedom.

All the West European parties lined up on the new Soviet positions with one notable exception—the PCI. In the period

53. Declaration of the Conference of Representatives of the Communist and Workers' Parties of the Socialist Countries (Moscow, 14–16 November 1957), Foreign Language Publishing, Moscow 1957.

following the 20th Congress of the CPSU and starting with Togliatti's interview with *Nuovi Argumenti* at the 8th Congress of the Italian Party, the leadership of the PCI began to develop an "Italian road" which already contained some of the essential themes of what we now know twenty years later as Eurocommunism—among them the interdependence of democracy and socialism, the need for political pluralism in the construction of socialism and the rejection of the Russian model in favour of organic ties to the real historic development of the nation. In the words of one of the leaders of the PCI at that time: "There was a doubt that we wanted to remove: the idea that the party intended to collaborate with other political forces and play according to the rules of the democratic game only up to the moment when it became necessary to make the 'leap' to the installation of the dictatorship of the proletariat and the building of socialism; and that from that moment on our policies would be more and more like those that had marked the dictatorship of the proletariat and the building of socialism in the Soviet Union. We tackled this misunderstanding openly."[54] This doubt or misunderstanding had been inherent in every different form that Communist strategy had taken in the struggle for democracy before 1956—in the Popular Fronts of the thirties and in the Anti-Fascist Unions of the forties. Even after the 20th Congress of the CPSU the doubt persisted, because the statements and practice of all the Western CPs (including the Italian) were contradicted by the declarations of the international communist movement to which they subscribed, as in the 1957 and 1960 conferences. They also failed to link any clear critique of the Eastern "models" to their stated national positions.

The PCF's opposition to Gaullist authoritarianism and the PCE's fight against the Franco dictatorship were also hindered by the same doubts, because both parties continued after the 22nd Congress to display an unconditional support for the Soviet Union which did not match their democratic objectives. In fact the PCF even launched a formal attack on

54. Giorgio Napolitano, in an interview with Eric Hobsbawm in *La Politique du parti communiste italien*, Paris 1976, p. 42.

the line adopted by the PCI at its 8th Congress (perhaps echoing the unspoken thoughts of the CPSU) and for ten years to come retained strong reservations about Italian "revisionism". It was not until the meeting between the two parties in November 1975, which found the French party aligned on Italian positions (apart from certain disagreements on international policy), that these reservations finally disappeared.

The evidence that emerged after the 20th Congress of the CPSU showed the dictatorship of the proletariat, as it had taken historic form in Eastern Europe, to be the very negation of democracy—not only of so-called "bourgeois democracy" but also of so-called "proletarian democracy". It forced the West European parties sooner or later to take a critical distance from Soviet models and to explore more deeply the problem of the relationship of democracy to socialism. At the same time, the 1950s and sixties saw general economic growth in the capitalist world and an increase in the military and economic might of the United States, while in the countries of the Soviet bloc continuing relative poverty, low productivity and serious economic and social disequilibrium belied the official figures of overall growth (of limited credibility, given the absence of any democratic control of them). This made the prospect of the Western parties coming to power as a result of the "socialist" system beating capitalism in "peaceful competition" appear less and less convincing. Even the start of a new general crisis of the capitalist system did not basically affect the situation, since it simultaneously aggravated the problems of the "socialist system".

With that prospect closed, the Western CPs turned definitively to the search for more solid national alliances and autonomous solutions. To do so they had to dissipate the "misunderstandings" about them and really come to grips with the problem of democracy. It was not only the outcome of "peaceful competition" that was uncertain—by now the two superpowers were tending towards a partnership to control the world, each respecting the other's vital zone of influence. The principal requirement of this US-Soviet peaceful coexistence, so far as Europe was concerned, was—and remains—maintenance of the *status quo*. Hence, as we have already mentioned, French and Spanish party criticisms of Soviet foreign policy.

The Chinese Cultural Revolution offered the promise, though not the achievement, of a complete alternative to the Soviet model and contributed to the further devaluation of the latter in the Western parties, without replacing it as the point of reference for strategy and tactics. Those small groups that did break from the traditional parties to create Maoist parties never developed further, since their concepts and practice were totally divorced from the realities of mature capitalism. Other small bands of communists chose—until they were expelled—to work within the official parties, trying to use the main ideas of the Cultural Revolution to enrich the critique of capitalism and Stalinism and the search for a new revolutionary strategy for the West. (The best example of this attitude was the *Manifesto* group in Italy.)

The revolutionary movements of the Third World, the Cuban revolution, the Latin American guerilla movements, the Algerian national liberation struggle, the revolutionary war in Vietnam, the Palestinian guerilla operations, all had a radicalising effect on sections of the European Communist parties and on those outside them, especially among youth, encouraging Left (and Leftist) criticisms of their routinism and their concentration on immediate objectives without any unifying strategic alternative.

The simplistic notion developed by Stalinist Marxism-Leninism that capitalism had been in a permanent state of crisis since the time of the October Revolution had so conditioned the Communist Parties that a Marxist analysis of the real dialectic of the capitalist imperialist system, of the changes it had undergone at every level, of the long period of expansion that followed the Second World War with its new forms of class struggle, were all quite beyond them. It was only very late, when the expansion was almost exhausted, that they got to grips with these questions. The European parties kept their heads down under the ideological effluvia of neo-capitalism, limiting themselves to support of trade union struggles (sometimes), winning seats in municipal councils and in parliament, and making abstract propaganda. But they were unable to develop a strategic perspective based on a real understanding of the national and international conjuncture, which would have had to include a thorough critique of Khruschev's neo-Stalinist regime, neo-capitalism and the effects on the West of the Third World Revolutions.

Against Gaullism and Christian Democracy, the French and Italian parties could manage only a day-by-day response with no perspective. The Spanish party had a more obvious general aim in its struggle against the Franco dictatorship and was able to develop some original initiatives, but it failed to understand the nature of the country's capitalist development and therefore the real nature and function of the Franco regime, with the result that it constantly suffered from illusions about the fragility and imminent downfall of the latter and conceived alliances that were not based on the real positions of the different class forces. In 1964 this produced a crisis within the party leadership, a minority raising some of the problems concerning the Soviet system, the new features of capitalism and the nature of the party which would be taken up by the official leadership again years later (though not the question of the party). Similar tensions and conflicts developed also in the PCF and PCI. After the death of Togliatti—who left a "Testament" in which he tried to lay a firmer foundation for the "Italian road to socialism"—a debate began around the radicalisation of the PCI's youth organisation, in which distinct currents emerged on the Left, Right and Centre of the party.

The Algerian war, Vietnam, the effects of the 20th Congress and the renewal of Marxism outside the party's ranks combined to produce a similar crisis in the PCF, affecting its student organisation and other elements. Thorez resisted even a Khrushchev-style destalinisation and expelled the Servin-Casanova group, but shortly before his death he too gave in and returned to the idea of a "socialism in the French style". This line was confirmed with the promotion of

Waldeck-Rochet to the post of General Secretary in 1964.

In the second half of the sixties all three parties, especially the French, experienced the growth of Far Left groups with substantial weight in the student milieu, and of new socialist currents in the political and trade union movement that claimed to represent an alternative to both the traditional social-democratic and communist parties. At the same period the debates on Marxism and the new developments in the social sciences that we noted above started to affect the CPs, showing up the theoretical poverty that had marked them since the days of the Communist International. This was reflected at the political level in the lack of any strategy fitted to the social formations of advanced capitalism. The "peaceful parliamentary road" that the CPSU had posited at the 20th Congress was fast disappearing and the only alternative to be found was in elements of the Italian party's policies.

It is this poverty that explains why all three parties were so taken by surprise by the events of 1968–9. The great social movements of Spring 1968 in France and Autumn 1969 in Italy suddenly put the need for a socialist transformation of the Western societies back on the agenda, showed what a surprisingly large social base aspired to such a transformation and simultaneously demonstrated that it was not going to be realised by keeping within the narrow limits and forms which confine democracy under bourgeois rule. These upheavals made it clear that the road to socialism lies through a deepening and enlarging of democracy in every sphere of political, economic, social and cultural life. At a certain point this must signify the transformation of all social relations, including those of production, and the transformation of power. We shall return shortly to the content of this demand for democracy; let us simply state here that it was posed by the mass movements of 1968–9 not just to society as a whole, but specifically to those political and trade union organisations that claimed to speak for socialism. The Communist Parties were questioned not only because of their lack of a strategy, but also because their very mode of being led them to act as brakes on the movement instead of developing and resolving its political potential. The PCI at least showed sufficient understanding to enable it to "ride the tiger", cleverly adapting to the forms of *democrazia di base* created by the initiative of students and workers, in order to moderate their dynamic more readily from within. The PCF by contrast clashed directly with the student movement, doing its best to set the working class against it.

The French May, the Italian Autumn and the invasion of Czechoslovakia—whose effect we have already discussed—constitutes a drastic challenge to the powerful French and Italian Communist Parties; they showed up how slow and routine were their responses and how many were the gaps in their theory. There was now mass criticism of them, conducted mainly by the youth, but also by advanced workers; healthy criticisms, although they occasionally fell into "infantile leftism" (senile conservatism can after all be a danger too). Thereafter the PCF, PCI, PCE and other West European parties intensified their efforts to improve their analysis of reality and adjust their strategy to it. The PCF took its first step with the adoption of the Champigny Manifesto by its Central Committee in December 1968. Then in 1972 it signed the Common Programme with the Socialist Party and the Left Radicals. The PCI developed its strategy of the "historic compromise" during 1973–4, while the PCE began work on its Manifesto and Programme in 1973. In the course of 1975 these parties arrived at the common formulation (first PCI-PCE, then PCI-PCF) of the "democratic road to socialism" in which the interdependence of democracy and socialism was the central concept.

We can summarise this brief outline of the vicissitudes in the relationship between democracy and socialism in the history of Marxism and of the workers' parties inspired by it in the following points:

1. With the development of capitalism and the consequent increase in the number of wage-earners, the old concept of democracy acquired a new meaning inimical to bourgeois rule. Marx and Engels in their theory of socialist revolution equated democracy with socialism and preached the struggle

for democracy as the principal axis of the struggle by the proletariat to achieve its own class rule.

2. From the beginning of the workers' movement social and economic struggles had always been indissolubly linked to the struggle for the democratisation of political and social structures.

3. Confronted by the growing strength of the proletariat and other exploited classes, the bourgeoisie was obliged to make concessions on the terrain of democracy but by the use of coercion and ideological hegemony restricted the workers' democratic gains within limits compatible with the continuing rule of the bourgeoisie.

4. One of the most effective stratagems of the bourgeoisie in maintaining its ascendency over the masses was its claim to a patent on democracy. Making a virtue of necessity, it transformed institutions wrung from it in struggle into the natural product of capitalist development, a bourgeois creation and ideal form of bourgeois state. Democracy thus appeared as a formal political mechanism devoid of class content, above class, ensuring harmony and cooperation between the classes. This ideal mirage was reinforced by the fact that the bourgeoisie was simultaneously obliged to make concessions to the workers' social and economic struggles. (These concessions were made possible by the development of the forces of production in the advanced capitalist countries—in part due to the pressure of workers' struggles—and by colonial exploitation.)

5. Experience of history shows that this form of ideological and political alienation—acceptance as a natural product of capitalism and expression of the democratic nature of the bourgeoisie of what are really victories of mass struggle against it—has had an extremely negative effect on the consciousness of the masses. It is also one of the ideological and political determinants of the division of the Marxist-inspired workers' movement into its two main currents. On the one hand the Social-Democratic current cherished ill-founded illusions in the solidity of partial democratic gains; on the other the revolutionary Communist current lapsed into a general under-estimation and distrust of democracy.

6. Social-democracy, or at least that right-wing variant that is hegemonic in most Socialist parties, simply takes over the notion of democracy diffused by bourgeois ideology. It views democracy simply as a mechanism which is equally well suited to capitalism or socialism, and assumes that democratic collaboration between the classes can effect a transformation from one system to the other. In its political practice Social-Democracy privileges electoral skills, social negotiations and such reforms as are compatible with capitalist interests. On every occasion it adapts its social goals to the limits imposed by bourgeois rule and in fact functions as an assistance rather than a hindrance to successive periods of modernisation and rationalisation of capitalism. Unable to eliminate conflicts, whether manifest or latent, between bourgeois rule and workers' democratic gains, social-democracy seeks to palliate them.

7. Born of the October Revolution, the Communist Parties were formed in a long period of direct struggle against Social-Democracy and "bourgeois-democracy", which profoundly shaped their politics and ideology. They tended to play into the hands of bourgeois ideology by identifying democracy with bourgeois rule. By counter-posing "proletarian" to "bourgeois" democracy they credited the idea that the bourgeoisie can be democratic. Since for a whole epoch the incarnation of "proletarian democracy" was a regime that denied the mass of workers the most elementary rights, the Communist Parties lent credence to the idea that democracy is only compatible with capitalism. The institutions in which the democratic gains of the masses had taken concrete form were used in a purely instrumental and tactical way, with the perspective that, after the conquest of power, they would be suppressed in favour of the Eastern model of "proletarian democracy". In the policy of the Popular Front the Communist Parties partly re-evaluated "bourgeois democracy", using it to accumulate forces and to forge new alliances, but only—until the turn of recent years—in the instrumental way we have indicated. In the practice of Social-Democracy as well as of the Communist Parties the concept of the "struggle for democracy" has involved a dis-

sociation between political action (reserved to the party) and action on social questions (reserved to the trade unions). Any form of democracy from below or grass-roots democracy that has a tendency to overcome this division between the political and the social has either been underestimated or directly opposed.

8. The historical experience of those CPs that have come to power shows that further industrialisation coupled with the elimination of private capital is quite insufficient for the creation of a socialist society. The result is as likely to be a new type of social regime, divided like its predecessor into rulers and ruled, in which cultural and national oppression, inequality and authoritarianism persist. It has been demonstrated that there can be no socialism without freedom and democracy.

Equally the history of capitalism, marked by colonial and imperialist wars, fascist and other types of dictatorship, gives ample evidence of a fundamental hostility between capitalism and democracy. Popular struggles alone explain the existence of certain elements of freedom and democracy, and these are in constant danger of confiscation if the interests of capital so demand and if mass resistance does not prevent it. Taken together the experience of both systems amply confirms the truth of the theoretical formulation of the founders of Marxism: the mutual dependence of democracy and socialism.

9. As the truth about East European "socialism" became more widely known the Communist Parties of capitalist Europe found themselves facing a crucial dilemma. It was impossible that the peoples of this region, formed in the struggle for freedom and democracy ever since the days of the great bourgeois revolutions, could ever accept that this kind of "socialism" was the goal of the anti-capitalist struggle. If they remained committed to the Eastern model they would be blocking any hope of political advance. Because of the weight of Stalinist "Marxism-Leninism" and of leaderships that had been formed in decades of practice within that ideology, there was a long and difficult path to travel before the rediscovery of the interdependence of democracy and socialism was formulated in the "democratic road". No sooner developed, the strategy now faces the rude test of the general social, political

and economic crisis in which the countries of the principal Eurocommunist Parties presently find themselves.

Eurocommunism's Anti-Monopoly Strategy

The contradiction between democracy and bourgeois rule grows sharper in the imperialist and monopolist phase of capitalism and is particularly exacerbated by the present conjunctural global crisis. Poulantzas has described some of the features of the State under monopoly capitalism that reflect this phenomenon.[55] We can summarise them as: an extreme concentration of power in the hands of the executive to the detriment of representative bodies such as parliament and municipalities; a confusion between the powers of the executive, legislature and judiciary, mainly characterised by the executive's intervention in the other two (for example police interference with justice); restrictions on rights and freedoms of the citizen to resist arbitrary action by the State; a decline of bourgeois political parties as the bureaucratic State administration takes over some of their functions of political organisation (this is true both for the working class and ruling blocs); a constant upgrading of the apparatus of state violence, both physical and ideological, and its increased use; establishment of new systems of "social control"; a distinction in every branch of the State apparatus (army, police, administration, judiciary and ideological apparatus) between formal open structures and small closed nuclei operating under tight control of the executive, real power being continually withdrawn from the formal to the informal structure (whereby the principle of public accountability disappears behind official secrecy); modification of the traditional concept of the "rule of law" by changes in the legal system and in the ideology of justice. These and other features all point in the same direction—an increase in repressive authority and a reduction in democracy.

55. Nicos Poulantzas, "Les transformations actuelles de l'Etat, la crise politique et la crise de l'Etat" in *La Crise de L'Etat*, Paris 1976, pp. 55–7.

In Western society this development of the State under monopoly capitalism is still partially concealed behind a certain democratic veneer, but in reality what democracy subsists is a function of the power of the workers' movement to resist the intrinsic tendencies of contemporary imperialism. Monopoly capitalism is now trying to change the balance of forces in its own favour, to break the resistance of the working-class and to resolve the crisis at its expense. Under monopoly capitalism any "anti-crisis" policy must be accompanied by an attack on democratic freedoms. The political apparatus required to impose an "austerity policy" necessarily includes the evolution of a repressive State to enforce the combination of unemployment and inflation, an increased tax burden, deteriorating social services, a higher rate of exploitation for those still in work, and a concentration and rationalisation of production which strikes not only at the wage-earners but also at small and medium-sized firms and the petty-bourgeoisie in trade, industry and agriculture.

The effects of this policy on the popular masses are contradictory. On the one hand it tends to polarise the great majority of wage and salary earners against the power of monopoly capitalism; from this point of view it provides an unprecedented objective basis for an anti-monopoly strategy based on the defence of democracy and its extension into every sphere of social and political life, including production, so that the demand for democracy becomes indissolubly linked to social and economic objectives—the nationalisation of monopoly capital, democratic planning, the direction of investment into areas of social need, full employment, agricultural development, industrial reconstruction, the need to adapt small firms to a new model of development.

On the other hand the kinds of "anti-crisis" policies imposed by monopoly capitalism also increase the inequalities and contradictions within society—between workers in jobs and the unemployed; over wage and salary differentials; between small businessmen and their employees; between city and countryside. The youth and women workers who make up the majority of the unemployed, and the students who see no career prospects, are particularly hard hit. The corporative defensive reactions that may result can induce exasperation, division and demoralisation; monopoly capitalism will use every political and ideological means to stir up such divisions, deploying repression against some and concessions to others.

There is no doubt that in the present historical conjuncture a correct strategy for a democratic road to socialism must involve pinning the main responsibility for the consequences of the crisis on the political and economic power of monopoly capital, showing it to be the principal enemy of the mass of the population and trying to group the great majority of the people around a policy designed to eliminate and replace it by democratic control centred on the working class. But a number of problems arise from the way in which the CPs of France, Italy and Spain have actually posed this strategy and sought to apply it. What is the essential content of their anti-monopoly strategy?

In the view of the three parties the democratic defeat of the political and economic power of monopoly capital by the majority of the population, under the hegemony of the working class, would still not constitute the beginning of socialism, but only of a long phase of *transition to socialism*—what the PCF refers to as "advanced democracy", the PCE as "political and social democracy" and the PCI as "a new stage in the democratic revolution". But in the traditional Marxist conception—which none of these parties has so far challenged—it is precisely this long transitional period between capitalism and classless society (or communism) which is called *socialism*, and which is initiated when the working class and its allies win power and take their first measures towards the social appropriation of the principal means of production. Now these are also the essential features of the "transition to the transition" which the Eurocommunists have introduced into their schema of the democratic road to socialism. Necessarily so, since monopoly capital is the determinant economic structure of the social formations of advanced capitalism, just as its State is the determinant politico-ideological structure, which at the same time intervenes decisively in the economy. It is therefore inevitable that a political and economic defeat of monopoly capital would have not merely an anti-monopoly but also an anti-capitalist significance, and would set in train a social process whose logic would be determined by the popular working-class nature of the new power which began to transform the State, by the existence of a large public sector of the economy corresponding to this new power and concentrating within it the basic means of production and other decisive aspects of the economy, and by the radical democratisation of every sphere of civil society. Whatever the inadequacies and limitations of the French Union of the Left's "Common Programme" or the PCE's programme of "political and social democracy", if effectively applied they would establish a transitional social formation with these characteristics. Why then deny the socialist nature of the process?

The PCI has as yet made no such concrete response, since its proposed "democratic stage" is much vaguer than the French or Spanish versions. It is presented rather as a gradualist process in which "elements of socialism" appear and the logic of capitalism begins to lose ground to another socialist logic. But the question of what conditions are required for these "elements" and "logic" to become the new dominant forms, and by what criteria one should judge whether or not socialism has arrived—is lost in the mists of the "historic compromise".

Some of the PCF's leading theoreticians have synthesised the 22nd Congress's account of the distinction between "advanced democracy" and socialism thus: "There is no Chinese wall between the phase defined by the Common Programme and the French version of socialism; socialism will be democracy carried through to its logical conclusion, that is to say the extension of social ownership under various forms to all the major units of production, commerce and services that are presently capitalist; the extension of democratic management and planning; the general raising of standards of information and culture; the affirmation of the capacities of the working-class within the political power of the labouring masses, and the possibility of further extending social emancipation by use of the twin democratic weapons—resolute struggle and universal suffrage."[56]

Obviously these are differences of degree, and it is difficult to see why they should constitute the definition of a properly *socialist* process rather than the qualitative rupture represented by the defeat of monopoly capital, and the coming to power of a coalition under the hegemony of the working class, which takes into social ownership the principal means of production.

What about the PCE? According to its "Manifesto and Programme",[57] "Political and social democracy will represent the passing into social ownership of the decisive economic and financial institutions that are today in the hands of the oligarchy. As such it will mark an advance of historic importance towards the socialisation of the means of production. But it will still not be socialism." The document goes on to make it plain that in political and social democracy small and medium-sized firms will continue under private ownership and there will therefore continue to be a bourgeois class enjoying legal status "which will naturally tend to strive for hegemony . . . (this) signifies that active class struggle will continue on every terrain within the society . . . To describe such a system as socialist would be to devalue socialism, which is more than just the social ownership of all the means of production and exchange—it is a new form of civilisation in which the level of development of the productive forces, of individual and collective consciousness, of relations of freedom and equality, are determined not merely by the nature of the class that exercises the leading position in power, but by the real changes that these classes have wrought in the economy, the social superstructure and collective consciousness".

56. Jean Fabre, François Hincker, Lucien Séve, *Les Communistes et L'Etat*, Paris 1977, p. 210.

57. Published as an undated pamphlet by the PCE together with the material from the Second National Conference.

Devaluing socialism? It is difficult to give any unambiguous interpretation of what the PCE might mean by this explanation. The omission from this stage, in contrast to the stage of "political and social democracy" of any reference to class struggle, might suggest that what they here refer to as "socialism" is what Marx understood as "communism". On the other hand they indicate that there will still be separate classes. Are we therefore talking about a form of socialism with classes but with no class struggle? A new Khruschevite, productivist version of socialism?

The continued existence of classes, including the petty and middle bourgeoisie, and of other elements of capitalism (such as the market, the capitalist division of labour etc) and therefore of struggle between them are properly features of socialism, which—like the State—will only disappear in the course of a long process of class struggle. They seem to provide no warrant for the Eurocommunist distinction between "advanced democracy" and socialism. We must therefore assume that other reasons, not clearly formulated, lie behind the distinction.

One possible reason could be mere propaganda—or rather publicity. On the principle of presenting merchandise in a wrapping suited to the mentality of the clientele, the aim would be to tranquillise the non-monopoly bourgeoisie on the assumption that it will be more likely to believe promises to respect its interests if they are presented under the label of an anti-monopoly "advanced democracy" rather than under the label of socialism. This idea is very clearly discernible in the 'Manifesto and Programme': "The working class promises to respect non-monopoly property in the stage of political and social democracy, in exchange for the support of the associated social forces in putting an end to big monopoly capital and its State power. In exchange for this guarantee of its social and political status the non-monopoly layers which are under pressure from the process of accumulation and concentration of wealth into fewer and fewer hands will join with the working class."

Another possible reason is the peculiar conception of

monopoly capitalism and its State generally prevalent among the Communist Parties, although with some recent corrections. (The PCI usually avoids the terminology, while retaining the conception.) According to this theory, capital is antagonistic not only to the working classes but also to all non-monopoly fractions of the bourgeoisie. No account is taken of the extent to which non-monopoly capital is organically integrated into the global system hegemonised by monopoly capital and operates, develops and reproduces itself as an intrinsic part of that system. In a period of crisis one simply sees in more concentrated form the normal dialectic of the system—intensified in periods of crisis—which constantly breaks up units of non-monopoly (and even of monopoly) capital while simultaneously reproducing or creating others. There are political and economic reasons, for monopoly capital to attend to the interests of smaller capital at the same time as it seeks to absorb it. In other words the two types of capital are at once antagonistic and complementary.

This ambivalent relationship is reflected also at the level of political power and the State. It is not the case, as the Communist Parties claim, that either is the expression *exclusively* of monopoly capital, rather they are the expression of a *power bloc* composed of different fractions of monopoly and non-monopoly capital, within which each strives for hegemony. Under monopoly capitalism the State is the institutional condensation of this power bloc (in political, ideological and organisational terms) and reflects the relationship of forces between its various components. It is similarly traversed and conditioned by the struggles and strength of the oppressed classes. In short the State enjoys a certain autonomy with respect to any class or fraction of a class among the ruling bloc, for only thus can it fulfil its essential task of ensuring the functioning reproduction of the system as a whole. In the PCF however the idea still obtains that: "The State together with the monopolies organically constitutes a single mechanism which controls every lever over society."[58] Similarly the PCE in its 'Manifesto and Programme' declares that the present

58. *Les Communistes et L'Etat*, p. 119.

form of the State is "the exclusive instrument of the monopolists". Starting from the reduction of the relationship between monopoly and small capital to one of simple antagonism, the Communist Parties deduce the possibility of the *entire* non-monopoly bourgeoisie allying itself to the working class in a struggle against the power of monopoly capital. In order to secure such an alliance they are obliged to guarantee that the new regime will not go beyond "anti-monopoly" limits.

A third possible reason for the introduction of a stage of "transition to the transition" lies in the conviction of the Communist Parties that they constitute *the* vanguard, *the* party of the working class, the sole custodians of "the scientific Marxist method". In the PCE's Manifesto-Programme we read that "history has confirmed that the possession of the method of scientific Marxism puts the Communist Party in a better position than any other workers' party *to lead the proletariat and its allies* in the fight for political power and the attainment of socialism".[59] In the view of the Communist Party it is only under Communist leadership that the working class can effectively achieve the hegemony which is a precondition for socialism. To soften the tension between this view and its alliance with the Socialist Party, the French Communist Party now uses the formula of "the leading influence". The proof of the pudding will be in the eating. According to the General Secretary of the French party one of the "iron laws" of socialism is "the leading influence of a vanguard party inspired by scientific socialism".[60] This too may be one of the motives for the introduction into Eurocommunist strategy of a "transition to the transition"—it will only be possible to pass from the "anti-monopoly transition" to the "socialist transition" after the Communist Party has fully conquered a "leading influence".

This problem of two stages in the advance of socialism may at first sight appear somewhat abstract and academic, but its

59. Manifesto-Programme, op. cit., p. 139, my emphasis.
60. G. Marchais, Report to the 22nd Congress of the PCF, in *Les PC Espagnol, Français et Italien face au pouvoir*, Paris 1976, p. 128.

consequences for Eurocommunist practice are of no small significance. We are already getting some indications of what it means in their short-term policies in relation to the ruling blocs hegemonised by monopoly capitalism. If the transition to socialism—the transition to the transition—means anything, it means *a period of uncertain struggle*, during which monopoly capital, though badly beaten, remains undefeated. That implies a period of the most acute class conflict since the defeat of monopoly capital would signal the inception of a process which would see the elimination of capitalism altogether and the start of the socialist transition. It is therefore unrealistic to conceive of any "advanced democracy" providing a long period of "democratic stability". It is equally illusory to look for any *stable* alliance with the *entire* non-monopoly bourgeoisie or with any political representatives of any fraction of monopoly capital—although it is of course essential to take advantage of inter-bourgeois contradictions and particularly to try to win the masses that are under bourgeois influence.

In a country such as France or Italy, the high rate of economic growth during the fifties and sixties might have lent some degree of credibility to the perspective of an "advanced democracy", though it would have implied a reformist co-existence with monopoly capitalism on the Swedish or West German model rather than its defeat. It would also have implied the complete social-democratisation of the Communist Parties. But in the present conjuncture of a global capitalist crisis such a perspective is absurd. Either the forces that are fighting for socialism will decisively establish their hegemony, or there will inevitably be a counter-revolutionary reversal—by which we do not, in the West European context, necessarily mean a Pinochet, though that possibility cannot be ruled out. This decisive phase is approaching in France and cannot be far away in Spain. In Italy it has already started.

In the present conjuncture nothing could be less prudent or more dangerous than a predominantly gradualist tactic (theoretically legitimated by reference to the "two stage" strategy) which is essentially centred on the political arena, especially on elections, and which subordinates all forms of mass action and social struggle to a quest for alliances with one or several fractions of the bourgeoisie (and we must not forget that the non-monopoly bourgeoisie comprises the greater part of the bourgeoisie and is responsible for the exploitation of a large part of the working class), for fear that such struggle will develop autonomous and unitary organisations of the working class and popular masses, thereby jeopardising the sacrosanct "leading role" of the Communist Parties.

I am not suggesting that the importance of the electoral struggle should in any way be underestimated. Quite the contrary. Democratic elections to representative assemblies at every level can both express the existing class balance and sometimes alter it. So long as elections do not indicate the existence of a fairly solid conscious majority in favour of radical change, the essential condition for a decisive confrontation with monopoly capitalism, whether in mass struggle or within representative bodies, is not fulfilled. But the more important indicator, particularly in a period of crisis, is the level of social struggle. It is here that the great majority of the population, which in the advanced capitalist countries means wage and salary earners and small independent producers, organises, unites and raises its consciousness though the practical experience of struggle for goals that represent a real alternative to capitalism. Such struggles not only represent a search for immediate solutions (however partial) to the most pressing problems—of wages, prices, working conditions, unemployment, housing, schools, transport or health. In every area and institution of civil society, every portion of the State apparatus, but especially in the workplace, they alter the balance of forces, assisting the growth of democratic socialist currents among employees, and even among the personnel of the military and repressive apparatuses. As we have seen, the stated positions of the French, Italian and Spanish parties emphasise the need for mass organisations and mass struggle, but their declarations are frequently belied by their practice. It is no accident that within the Communist Parties and the trade union groups in which they exercise hegemony criticisms of this practice are multiplying. Such criticisms can only be raised in concrete circumstances, and are not part of our present task. What we do wish to suggest is that for all the reasons we have given a strategy of two stages tends to produce a dissociation of the social struggle from the political struggle—very much in the Communist tradition—and to give primacy to the political, and within that to the electoral arena, with a tendency to play down working class self-organisation and struggles which might upset alliances with the "non-monopoly bourgeoisie". We wish to underline the dangers inherent in this tendency during a period of heightened class struggle such as the present, when every day the choice between monopoly capitalism or democratic socialism is posed more starkly. Italy provides an eloquent illustration of the dangers.

The Italian Test

As the PCI comes ever closer to participation in government, and as the "historic compromise" dwindles towards a "creeping compromise", there is much doubt and disquiet in the ranks of the first of the Western parties. Disquiet about the turn the social-political process has taken, doubt about the present party line. This uneasiness has now spread from the base to the leadership of the Italian Communist Party. By October 1976 members of the Central Committee, among them Luigi Longo the Party's President, had begun to voice the question which was being heard ever more frequently among the masses—Are the sacrifices that the workers are being asked to accept really going to produce key reforms or are they merely going to reinforce monopoly capitalism and its servitor Christian Democracy? In a veiled criticism of Berlinguer's leadership, Longo warned: "in trying to solve everything by arrangements and calculations made at the top, it is possible the party could lose contact with the real struggle, at the base, where its strength lies."[61] Already at that time important sections of workers who had begun to oppose the tactics of the PCI and its supporters in the trade union leaderships were accusing them of making concessions to the Andreotti "austerity programme" without winning any of their own demands in return.

So far, by the use of strikes and other defensive struggles, the employed members of the Italian working-class have succeeded in fending off the worst attacks on their standard of living. At the same time the situation of the great mass of unemployed workers, largely women and young people, has worsened; for hundreds of thousands of students there is no prospect of a job. Amongst these layers there is a growing mistrust of the traditional Left-wing organisations both in party politics and in the unions. The most spectacular demonstration of this process was the student revolt of February-March 1977, but a similar attitude is spreading within the "marginalised" sections of the proletariat. As a close observer of the Italian political scene who is sympathetic to the PCI put it, "if things carry on the way they are going there will be two Italies cohabiting in the peninsula: one the institutional Italy within which the Communist Party makes its slow but steady progress; the other the real Italy where among marginalised citizens, women, unemployed and students, life becomes daily harder and the Communists have become *persona non grata*".[62]

In March 1977, with the student revolt scarcely over, the PCI Central Committee met in an atmosphere charged with tension and alarm. Gian Carlo Pajetta, one of the main leaders of the party, described the conjuncture as "a complicated situation, bristling with difficulties, full of hidden dangers."[63] For Cesare Luporini the youth rebellion had shown "how slow and ill-prepared the Party has been in channelling molecular processes and explosive contradictions . . . A beam of society has fallen and hit us on the head, let us take care the

61. *L'Unità*, 21 October 1976.
62. Marcelle Padovani, in *Le Nouvel Observateur*, 25 April 1977.
63. *L'Unità*, 16 and 17 March 1977.

same does not happen with other pieces . . . It was out of an empty future and a desire to seize what is available right now that the rebellion was born, out of a sense of being on the edge of society which leads to a lack of confidence in organised forms of democracy . . . We Communists are identified by the students as "co-managers" of the present society rather than as the bearers of a new order". Another member of the Central Committee (Lucio Lubertini) declared: "Many people, more than those who voted for us, have invested great hopes in the PCI and the Left: the hope of a real change in Italian society. If their hopes remain unfulfilled too long, the danger is not that we lose control of the consensus to Left extremism, but rather—as has happened before in this century in Germany, France, Italy and elsewhere—that society as a whole moves to the Right. What has occurred in the university is a warning of a much wider problem . . . To assume that if things get difficult we can always simply return to opposition and renew our ties with the masses, shows no understanding of the real problem; we have chosen our road and we cannot turn back from it without suffering some loss. We are now in an impasse. Either we force a way through, or we suffer a historic defeat. But the only way to get through is to ensure that the level and achievement of mass struggle keep in step with political advances."

"Are we still basically a party of struggle?" It was Armando Cossuta who gave voice to this question, which lay behind the whole proceedings of the Central Committee. Ever since the Second World War Togliatti has described the PCI as "a party of struggle and a party of government". During its long period in opposition after 1947, while it waited for an opportunity to prove again the truth of the second epithet, the first had never been in question. Since the adoption of a tactic of conditional support for the Andreotti government the question has been heard more frequently. Pajetta echoed it in his own speech: "It must be made absolutely clear that we are not *in* the government, we are not the government; that on the contrary we consider this government quite unable to meet the needs of the country. We are certainly ready to assume our full measure of responsibility, but we shall do so by demonstrating that we are at the same time a party of government and a party of struggle." . . . "To engage the movement in a deliberate united battle, the party must be *within* the movement." He emphasised that the present political context "is only valuable to us in so far as it allows a new situation to mature".

Although the majority of the Central Committee shared the positions of Pajetta, they were clearly opposed by Amendola, representing the Right of the Party, who called for "a clear opposition to extremism, which today represents the main enemy for the workers' movement and its political line . . . (and which) shares common features with fascism". For Amendola this was not the moment to change the party's attitude to the government. The party should give more whole-hearted support for the "austerity" policy—when it was precisely the capitalist nature of the austerity policy that was responsible for the alarming phenomena of marginalisation and social decomposition.

Berlinguer was not present for the debate, due to a well-timed indisposition. However, the speeches of some of his "supporters" dismayed the majority—especially their tendency to rely on the repressive agencies of the State to restore the public order jeopardised by the revolt of the students or other marginalised sectors. It was Giorgio Napolitano who summed up the main political conclusion of the debate, which has since been reflected in policy decisions by the PCI. "We must move rapidly beyond the political balance of forces that was defined by the legislative elections of June 20th". This meant abandoning the policy of parliamentary abstention, for an effort to reach agreement with Christian Democracy and other "constitutional" parties to constitute an "emergency" majority with a common programme, although without the PCI being directly represented in the government.

But in spite of this step and some significant clues in certain contributions to the debate, the Central Committee had no answer to the more general and insistent question about the PCI's strategic line. Why was it, after years of spectacular

electoral successes, after winning control of major cities and
regions, after penetrating the State apparatus, after securing
35% of the vote (47% taken together with the rest of the
Left) and effectively entering the governing majority—why
had the great social bloc the party had assembled so rapidly
begun to fall apart? Why was democracy now in danger? Why
was the previous confidence of party members and masses
now giving way to doubts?

One of the clues to which Luporini alluded was the party's
inability to respond to the great clamour for an alternative
approach that had come out of the movement of 1969.
Borgna pointed to the party's preference for defending the
existing limits of politics rather than for developing the conditions from which to surpass them. That is indeed a problem
of much longer date than just the period since the June 1976
elections.

As we said before the PCI had managed to "ride the storm"
in 1969 with a better sense of tactics than the PCF, but still
with the same general intent—not to direct the mass movement towards the option of a global alternative, but to act as a
brake, limiting the growth and autonomy of workers' self-
organisation, channelling it into the constraints of in-
stitutionalised politics so there should be no conflict between the two. The movement had created its own organs of
grass-roots democracy—factory councils, neighbourhood
councils, committees of the unemployed, of soldiers and
NCO's, committees for the "auto-reduction" of charges on
public transport, electricity and telephones, autonomous
movements among magistrates, doctors, journalists, police.
All these put forward specific anti-capitalist goals of struggle.
Unlike its counterparts in other European countries, this
movement in Italy did not wear itself out. It has now existed
for nearly ten years. But it has yet to deploy its full potential.
The PCI, which is the main political force within the movement, has not proposed that it should. At first there was no
objective contradiction between the new forms of grass-roots
democracy and the traditional forms of the workers' movement. On the contrary, the combination of the two made for a

more organic development of the new alternative social bloc. But of course the forms and aims of democracy from below imply the rejection of the formal legal limits set by the existing political system and contain within themselves the seed of the necessity to break with the old order and to compose a new. The strategy of the PCI assumes the respect of those existing limits. Gramsci's notion of "the war of position" has been constrained ever more tightly into a gradualist mould, whose perspective excludes any "rupture" or "qualitative leap".

In spite of Berlinguer's repeated rejection of accusations of gradualism, legalism and parliamentarianism, as the crisis of Italian society has become more severe the PCI, ever fearful of any "adventure", has put more and more emphasis on the gradualist and legalist tendency in its policy. Its activity has become more clearly concentrated around conventional political institutions, subordinating every surge of the workers' movement to the alliances and arrangements of the party at the political level.

The proposal to Christian Democracy of a "historic compromise", as a new stage of the "democratic revolution" (which according to the PCI version had merely been interrupted in 1947 by the Cold War), was to be the culmination of this strategy. In the articles with which he launched the initiative in 1973, Berlinguer defined the main goal of the "historic compromise" as the achievement of a consensus of much more than 51% of the population for the idea of a socialist transformation of society, to avoid the division of the country into two equal parts and a confrontation between them. The main lesson that Berlinguer drew from the Chilean tragedy and from other previous cases (among which he possibly had in mind Spain in the thirties) was the need to avert such a contingency. Can there be any principled objection to such a sensible proposal? The whole problem lies in how to achieve it. The PCI's ambition is evidently to sweep away the barrier of anti-communist sentiment which the Church and Christian Democracy have used against it for 30 years—and which is now anyway much diminished—to enable the Left to get closer to the Catholic masses organised or influenced by the DC. Its aim is to aid what Togliatti called the "popular soul" of Christian Democracy to prevail over its "reactionary soul", and thereby to change the balance of forces towards the formation of a great consensus for a peaceful, democratic advance towards socialism.

But in politics all roads do not lead to Rome, even if they may lead to control of its municipality. The PCI has sought to reach its goal by means of an understanding with Christian Democracy as a whole, therefore by way of its bureaucratic leadership, the main political instrument of Italian capitalism. The PCI thereby ran the risk of losing its own revolutionary soul to the devil, rather than saving the democratic soul of the DC.

What is the basis for the question that is presently troubling the PCI—whether it is still a party of struggle? To seek a far-reaching agreement—a *historic* compromise—with the main political instrument of Italian capitalism, especially in conditions of economic crisis when capitalism needs to adopt policies that are clearly anti-working class, can only result in the PCI, and those union leaderships it influences, trying to tone down both the aims and the methods of mass struggle, to restrict its demands for reform to the limits compatible with the system, to advocate these only at the level of propaganda without organising any real offensive to win them. The PCI thereby will limit its possibilities of developing a real pro-grammatic alternative to the way in which the DC and mono-poly capitalism proposed to solve the crisis. Yet at the same time the PCI has become the pole around which ever broader sections of the population focus their hopes; increasing its votes and winning control of some of the major regions of the country and most of its main cities. In office the PCI has provided a more efficient and honest management than the DC, but it has always kept within the limits and rules of the system, subordinated everything to the principal aim of further-ing the "historic compromise" with its great rival. This has naturally made it very difficult, if not impossible, for it to use those areas of power it has won within the institutions of representative democracy and the State machine to assist the organisation of struggle among those sectors that are hardest hit by the crisis—the unemployed, students, women; to unify these sectoral struggles with the struggles of the employed workers; to develop organs of rank and file democracy through which the masses could play a more active and direct part in solving their own problems; or to co-ordinate such organs with the institutions of representative democracy so that an electoral majority could become an active, fighting majority, with a growing awareness of its social role and tasks.

In short, in spite of the PCI's growing electoral success and its progressive "occupation" of positions of power in the political system, it has not managed to build up a social bloc that would be capable—in terms of consciousness, internal organisation or programme—of tackling the grave problems that are now imminent in Italy. For if it is true that one of the lessons of Chile and of previous revolutions is that a large majority conscious of its goal is necessary for a sure progress towards socialism, another no less important lesson is that the ruling classes and their state machine will not sit idly by while the working class bloc acquires that large majority—unless they are confident that the parties and trade unions that represent that bloc have no intention of changing any of the basic features of the capitalist system. (Social-democratic parties have sometimes been allowed to achieve this kind of large majority, but Communist Parties still do not enjoy the same degree of trust on the part of the capitalists—while some of the Socialist Parties have been losing the trust they used to inspire.) At any rate, we are working on the assumption that the PCI and the other Eurocommunist Parties do really wish to make the transition to socialism.

If a socio-political bloc genuinely intent on socialism shows by its electoral results under universal suffrage that it is close to achieving a democratic majority, the ruling classes will increasingly have recourse to undemocratic procedures to block its further advance. These may include economic sabotage, provocative acts by the repressive apparatus of the State or para-State bodies, diversionary manoeuvres in the realm of ideology—the range available is endless. It must also be remembered that any economic crisis cuts both ways. On the one hand, it aggravates contradictions between the ruling class and the oppressed, increasing the pressure for a democratic socialist alternative; on the other hand, as the Italian situation so dramatically demonstrates, it also exacerbates contradictions within the working class, making room for new ruling class manoeuvres. That is not to speak of a situation in which a Left social bloc actually comes to power legally by a democratic vote and then starts to take effective steps in the direction of socialism. In such a case the anti-democratic procedures listed above would merely be preparatory to the final argument of armed force.

The Eurocommunists are clearly right to say that the greater the consensus of support the socialist forces enjoy, both before and after their advent to power, the more difficult it will be for the forces of reaction to resort to any kind of violent action. But there is a vicious circle here, because it is therefore logical for the reactionaries not to wait until the left achieves that decisive consensus. In other words, there is no way to avoid what we have called the *period of uncertainty*, of extreme agitation in the class struggle during which the question not merely of government but of power comes to the fore. Two conditions must be fulfilled if the decision expressed by a broad majority of the population through universal suffrage is to take effect—it must be secured against the violence of the defeated parties, and it must be assured of the means of its own expression. The struggle within parliament and other representative bodies must be backed up by mass struggle in every sphere of social and political life, in the State apparatus, and the system of production. If that is to happen it is essential that organs of rank and file democracy should be developed and that they be co-ordinated with the organs of representative democracy. This is the only way that the alliance between the traditional working class, the new salaried layers and the other sectors (peasantry, traditional urban petty-bourgeois etc) to be incorporated into the alternative social bloc can be cemented. If this bloc is to cohere it will be around a clearly anti-monopoly (and therefore anti-capitalist) programme which combines the immediate measures demanded by the crisis with radical medium-term changes that give a clear idea of the intended future, and set in train a new logic of development that will progressively displace the logic of capitalism.

But is all this feasible if, as the PCI strategy would have it, the main axis for the construction of this new bloc lies in a long-term compromise with the main political representative of monopoly capital? Obviously the popular forces that are presently controlled by Christian Democracy have to be won to the new bloc—but are not those sections of the Italian Left (including some within the PCI) correct, who say that this goal will only be achievable when there has been a scission within the CD between its popular democratic sectors and the political layer that serves monopoly capital? Many observers of the Italian situation have reported that, far from weakening the grip of the Christian Democratic leadership, the policy of a "historic compromise" as conceived and carried out by the majority leadership of the PCI, has actually helped to strengthen it and to slow down the rate at which elements of the Catholic movement were breaking away to Left positions—given that the PCI ascribes a capacity for a genuinely popular politics to the DC leadership.

The mighty Italian Communist Party is at a crossroads today. Not a few now believe that the most likely outcome of its democratic road will be a role analogous to that of the British Labour Party or German Social-Democracy—mere collaboration with Christian Democracy to administer the crisis and carry through yet another rationalisation of the decrepit machinery of capitalism. The only difference would be that for such a function to be exercised in a country like Italy, a Noske-style repression would have to be unleashed against the workers' movement. That would be impossible without profound splits and rents in the fabric of the party.

This is not in our opinion the most probable outcome. The Italian workers' movement has a rich history of struggle and has repeatedly demonstrated its combativity and creativity.

Already there are signs within its ranks of a vigorous reaction to the dangers that threaten it and Italian democracy. The same is also true of the PCI, which possesses very close links with the masses and the workers' movement and is very sensible to pressure from them. Italian Communism exercises a degree of influence and political control within all the structures of Italian society (whether social or political, economic or cultural) which is greater even than its one third share of the vote would indicate. If we add to it the forces that are represented by the Socialist Party, the New Left and the democratic working-class sections of the Catholic world, we have not merely a numerical majority but also the most conscious, capable and active elements of the Italian population. The crucial need today on which any successful solution to the crisis depends, is to formulate a policy that unites all these forces in action for a thoroughgoing transformation of the country, which accepts the inevitability of a show-down with the present ruling group that represents monopoly capital, which seeks not merely to defend democracy but to advance it beyond its present inadequate limits, and to set in train a non-capitalist logic of development.

If this great task is to be accomplished, as we can discern from the debates within the PCI and outside it, a new strategy for the principal party of the Italian Left is an urgent necessity. Between the adventure of extremism and the adventure of the "historic compromise" (understood as collaboration with the forces that constitute the most fundamental block to the kind of change the present situation demands), space must be found for a realistic policy of advance towards the democratic socialist transformation of Italian society. The tempo of the crisis does not allow for a very long delay.

The Democratic Road the Only Possible Road

The preceding criticisms of certain aspects of the PCI's policies do not, of course, put in question the principle of a democratic road to socialism, which we regard as the only route open for the advanced capitalist countries. What we contest is the legalist, electoralist, gradualist version of that road; the version which seeks to follow a line of class collaboration with the leading group of the bourgeoisie. We have spent some time on the Italian example because it is there that the global crisis of capitalism has first reached a critical point and where already the costs of this version can be seen to be dangerously high; it therefore represents a warning not just to the Italian Left but also for the Left in France and Spain where a similar opportunist version of the democratic road also has its supporters, both within and outside the Communist Parties.

In reality the principle of a democratic road to socialism is universal. But in those so-called backward countries where the proletariat is still a small minority and the productive forces are at a low level it is still inevitable (as it was in the past) that there will be intermediate revolutions of another type, even though they call themselves socialist, which will have to make their own "assaults on the Winter Palace", wage their own guerilla wars or revolutionary wars, and pass through stages of state capitalism or some other form of socio-political system divided between ruling and ruled classes, which may neither properly be called capitalist nor properly socialist—as has happened with the Soviet Union and similar cases. When once they have reached a certain level of development all of these systems will have to confront the question whether it is really possible to build socialism without democracy. It is not by chance that this is the immediate and central concern of the socialist oppositions in the countries of Eastern Europe.

For the advanced capitalist countries we can say that the conditions are *objectively* ripe for a socialist way out of the capitalist crisis. In the first place the process of accumulation and concentration of capital has deprived the great majority of the population of all private ownership in the means of production, yet bestowed on them a long tradition of struggle for democratic rights. Their partial victories in this struggle have secured them a generally high cultural level. That majority is now in the position to demand and to *understand* a project of socialist transformation. In the present crisis both need and understanding will become more acute. The same mechanism of accumulation and concentration of capital has produced a high level of socialisation of production and of human needs that objectively demand collective management and planning.

But these two powerful objective conditions do not automatically lead to socialism, and could quite well (at least for a longish historical period) find their solution in a social system such as the fictional societies portrayed by Orwell or Zamyatin, which are not capitalist but are also the opposite of socialist. Such a result is possible not only because no objective tendency ever leads automatically to its corresponding social development, but also because there are contradictory elements within those very objective conditions to which we refer that could equally well serve as a basis for either alternative. The kind of socialisation which capitalism promotes in production, in the methods of production, in science and technology, are not perfectly adapted to socialism; they are also in part suited to an authoritarian type of regime, based on the regimentation of the masses who have been dispossessed of the means of production by a class of technocrats or functionaries—a "robot society" which could enjoy a high technology without an atom of freedom. Important elements of such a system are present already, not only in the regimes of Eastern Europe, but also in the most developed forms of monopoly capitalism. If the present global crisis is resolved at the expense of the working people, it would enhance the weight of these tendencies.

To arrive at socialism it is necessary that a majority of the population should not merely objectively need socialism and understand what it means, they must also be subjectively ready to enter actively into *struggle* to achieve it. While the winning of such a majority through the ballot box is a necessary condition, it is not a sufficient one for victory, since all history shows that no ruling class will ever voluntarily submit in face of a real threat to their position. Such classes are anti-democratic by their very nature. Hence the need to organise an electoral majority into a solid, non-atomised force—what we have referred to as a socio-political bloc: a bloc united around a common programme and strategy, and capable of meeting any circumstance that arose.

The first problem lies in the social heterogeneity of the majority that is objectively interested in socialism, constituted by classes and groups with their own contradictions. The social web of advanced capitalism is extremely complex. Alongside the traditional working class, which is differentiated into many layers, are the new layers of salaried personnel which play an ever more important part in the economy and society through their function in services and the organisation of production; they too are differentiated essentially into an upper elite whose interests are closely tied to those of capital, and a mass whose relationship to capital is similar to that of the proletariat, although it does not directly produce surplus value. Differences in their roles in the organisation of work and division of labour, differences of social status, culture and life-style can all create contradictions between the traditional working class and these salaried layers. Although their specific weight is less than it was, there are still important strata of petty-bourgeois proprietors in industry, agriculture and commerce who could and should be integrated into a process of socialist transformation which offered them the chance to improve their situation. These strata are not so important in the Anglo-Saxon countries, but are still significant in France and more so in Italy and Spain. There are other categories, too, which cannot be grouped under any particular class or layer but are increasingly important: women, students and youth in general. To which one could add, in a prolonged period of structural crisis such as we are in today, all those who are excluded from the productive process by unemployment.

Within this motley collection it is still the traditional working class whose radical antagonism to capital, whose role as producer of surplus value and whose powerful political parties and trade unions, make it the solid force with the greatest revolutionary potential and the natural hegemonic pole of any bloc of the oppressed. But as the salaried layers' antagonism to capitalism increases and their class-consciousness and socialist commitment grows they will have a more important role to play in establishing a popular hegemony.

For this large objectively anti-capitalist majority to be transformed into a subjectively socialist majority will demand a system of multiple, shifting alliances and convergences—not just alliances between political parties but also trade-unions and other mass movements and organisations; various forms of rank and file democracy and forms of representative democracy in parliament, municipalities. There are no objective grounds for counterposing one of these components to any of the others, and to do so can only delay the process of getting to grips with the extreme complexity of the socio-political reality. Of course the relative weight of the various components—the political parties, the trade unions, the organs of representative and grassroots democracy—will vary according to the real circumstances of the class struggle, the present margin of democracy and historical traditions, the combination of forms may be very diverse from country to country. But each element has its own specific contribution and its own limitations. Parties cannot substitute for trade unions and vice versa. Representative democracy cannot substitute for rank-and-file democracy, or vice versa. No class organisation can fulfill the role of the women's liberation movement or the student movement—and so on.

But there is one among this complex of structures within the workers socio-political bloc which is especially well fitted to perform the function of synthesis, of overall analysis and of formulation of strategy and tactics—and that is the party as Gramsci conceived of it, as a collective intellect. But not a *single* political party. It is inevitably in any class society, and especially in those as complex as the advanced capitalist countries, that there should be some political and ideological pluralism—not only as a function of society's division into hostile classes, but also because of the heterogeneity within those classes and layers. Even within the more homogeneous social groups such as the traditional working class there will inevitably exist a variety of political options. We have only to look at history for the evidence. *The* party of the working class is a myth. The reality is rather *the working class as a party*, meaning the totality of forms through which the class organises itself and expresses its class antagonism to the bourgeoisie (parties, unions, cultural organisations etc). The synthesising function, the development of a general orientation, a strategy and tactics for the entire socio-political bloc, can only adequately be exercised by a *political alliance* of a very diverse kind. Political parties will of course play a major role within the alliance, and whatever force best represents the interests of the class in the widest sense will exercise hegemony.

Now if parties are properly to fulfill their function of representing and mediating the totality of social forces within the bloc, they must have very close links to the different social groups, must be sensitive to the pressures and influence of the various organs of rank and file and of representative democracy, and of the mass organisations.

The political parties that are to represent the working class and other popular forces must then be truly democratic, subject to the criticism and control of the masses. In spite of a certain positive evolution of late, the self image and internal structure of the Communist Parties do not answer to these criteria and are poorly suited to the task of constructing such a socio-political bloc of the oppressed.

Throughout history no class or social group has ever developed an effective social bloc according to a predetermined schema, but only out of real struggles. (Indeed our description of the components of such a bloc is simply an abstraction from what has occurred in practice, a model for initiating future struggles.) Yet of course every kind of struggle is not equally useful in constructing a social bloc. Any narrowly corporative struggle can on the contrary isolate the participants from their objective allies. Whether the original demand is of a social, cultural or economic kind, if it is to serve a unitary function it must be associated to political demands.

Many factors militate against struggles serving to unite the people—each sector will have different priorities for immediate reforms, the ruling class takes care to separate claims and to play one off against the other, to divide and rule. If they are to assist in developing the socialist orientation of the socio-political bloc, struggles of any sector for its own immediate goals must be expressed as steps on the road to more far-reaching goals. Within the Communist Parties (and other Left parties) there is a tendency to regard overall political action as a private reserve and to try and restrict other organisations—the trade unions, organs of grassroots democracy, the women's movement etc—each to their own "specific problems", preventing them from taking political initiatives in relation to major general questions. This tendency reflects a submission to the dominant ideology which would present politics as the preserve of specialists; it can only hinder the construction of a socio-political bloc with a programme, strategy and organisational cohesion capable of vanquishing the resistance of the ruling class and taking the democratic road towards socialism. Because, if it is not to get bogged down in "improving" capitalism the workers' bloc must set as its central goal the achievement of political power, to enable it to undertake the necessary structural changes in the State and the economy. It is difficult to separate the two within an advanced capitalist society where the State is deeply involved in the economy as well as every sphere of civil society and the economy in turn has a profound effect on the structure of the State.

It is inadequate to limit proposals for dealing with the socio-economic structure to a progressive social appropriation of the present means of production—as the Eurocommunist Parties generally do. The means of production and also science and technology must be transformed to correspond to new relations of production. For it is false to see science and technology, the organisation and division of labour, as *neutral* agencies that can be equally well integrated into a capitalist or a socialist pattern of productive relations. They too must be transformed, revolutionised. Although the whole process may take a long time, the experience of a number of frustrated revolutions shows that it must at least be initiated right at the start of the transitional period. During the phase in which the working class bloc is still struggling for power it is possible, in addition to making a theoretical exposition of the problem, to achieve certain limited advances in this area: by opposing authoritarianism and aspects of the organisation of work within the factories, by developments of science and technology that are directed towards the satisfaction of social consumption, by a struggle to preserve the environment, and so on.

On the crucial question of conquering political power and transforming the State, the strategy of the Eurocommunist Parties is to win progressively more posts in the present State structures by a combination of electoral activity and mass struggle—in practice usually putting the emphasis on the former. Once a Left coalition has been brought to government by means of the ballot-box on a programme of "a transition to socialism", it will carry that programme through by democratising the institutions and machinery of the State. Whatever argument there may be over these parties' theoretical concept of the nature of the State under monopoly capitalism, this strategy seems to me to be well founded—provided it does not fall into the illusion of expecting the process to be entirely gradual, without any critical clash with the ruling class, without any qualitative break; and as long as it is clear that democratisation does not simply mean a change of personnel, but involves structural changes in the machinery of the State and in its links with civil society, in the direction of increased popular control.

In this strategic conception the decisive shift in the balance of class forces in favour of the new socio-political bloc would result from the combination of a number of different factors. These would include the development of democratic socialist currents within the ideological and repressive apparatuses of the State, which can proceed quite far in the former—particularly in the case of the educational system—and can at least impede or help to make more difficult the use of the latter against the will of the people; the winning of a majority in the parliament and other representative bodies, and therefore also in the government; and the growth of all manner of democratic socialist forces *outside* the apparatuses and institutions of the State.

Given the complexity of State and society within advanced capitalism, the diversity of "centres of power", the single decisive confrontation which was the model of past revolutions (which would not necessarily involve an armed clash in today's context) seems less likely. There is still room for discussion, but the most likely guess is that a decisive shift in the balance of forces would result from a *series* of clashes and partial breaks. It is not easy, in analysing previous revolutions, to locate the "decisive clash" with any precision. In the Russian Revolution, was it what Lenin once referred to as the *coup d'audace* in October or the Red Army's victory in the Civil War? The basic difference between a revolution in a backward country and a revolution in one of the advanced capitalist countries of Western Europe lies in the fact that if there is to be a revolution at all in the latter it will only be made when there is a majority that is both objectively and subjectively committed to socialism. That requires the existence of a social bloc which is able, because it comprises all the essential vital elements of society, to impose the kind of democratic process we have described. But we insist that it would be illusory to suppose that such a process could be purely evolutionary and to write off any risk of armed clashes. Of course the socialist forces will seek if possible to avoid such clashes, and to impose a peaceful transition from the beginning to the end of the process by democratic means—but it does not depend on them alone.

Not only in the period leading up to the assumption of political power, but also and especially in government, one of the essential elements in assuring cohesion to the bloc of the oppressed will be its programme. The programme of the bloc must combine immediate measures that deal effectively with present problems, with far-reaching reforms that can harmonise the varied sometimes contradictory interests of its different social components, within a coherent dynamic of democratic socialist transformation. All previous examples suggest that the decisive test for the programme will come in the field of the economy. So closely inter-related is every element of the economy within advanced capitalism that an interruption of production or distribution within one sector will produce an intolerable disruption throughout the system, unless it sets in motion a new logic of development capable of ensuring continuity of production and a prompt perspective of improved conditions for the majority of the people—especially since the ruling class, although removed from government, will only partly have been dislodged from power and will seek to take advantage of the turmoil that must inevitably result from any basic economic change to pin the blame for it on the political economy of the popular bloc. That will be the main weapon with which it will seek to detract sections of the masses away from the popular bloc and draw them back into the reactionary bloc.

The problem of how to make the necessary structural changes within a "coherent" political economy that can "open the way to socialism" is critical to the present debates in the French Left about the future application of the Common Programme. In Italy there is a similar debate over the urgent need to develop a programme of the same type that can include immediate "emergency" measures which are required by the gravity of the Italian crisis within the framework of a new logic of development that will break with the logic of capitalism.

The problem has not yet been posed so pressingly in Spain, where (at least in its own mind) the Left is still far from power. The economic policies advocated by the traditional parties of the Left are essentially located within the framework of capitalism. It may be objected, however, that they lack coherence in the sense that some of their policies are objectively incompatible with a *capitalist* solution of the crisis, whatever their intentions may be. Yet at the same time they do not pretend to offer any complete anti-capitalist alternative; in this respect as in so many other matters in the present political process in Spain they are neither fish nor fowl.

What of the Eurocommunist claim that democratic socialist forces can begin the process of "democratisation of the State" during the process of struggling for power and complete it when they have taken power? It is not enough to remove the top personnel from office in the various institutions of the State or to introduce a more democratic system of selection of such personnel, since it is the needs of monopoly capitalism that those institutions have been designed to meet (even if they have been modified to a greater or lesser extent by the struggle of the dominated classes). If the people are really going to play a part in the representative bodies of the State and control the product of their own labour, these institutions will have to be changed. The masses will also need access to a reliable system of information on major problems.

While it is essential to maintain and develop the traditional organs of representative democracy as a guarantee of the democratic process, it is equally important, if there really is to be greater participation by the people, to develop multiple forms of democracy from below, in mass movements and organisations. The two systems must be combined to provide the greatest possible degree of popular control within the nationalised industries and other sectors of production that have been taken into some form of social ownership, as also within all the basic services, and the institutions of social and cultural life. Through this combination a system of self-management could be progressively created at every level, co-ordinated by a flexible general plan which sets out basic options that have been scientifically delineated and democratically decided. Obviously such a process of democratisation of the State will include decentralisation and autonomy for local, regional or (where they exist) national entities.

In general the idea of democratisation of the State that is prevalent within the Eurocommunist parties is distorted by the ideology and tradition of "democratic centralism", which has come to be applied not only to the party, but to the organisation of society in general, with the element of "centralism" taking precedence over that of "democracy". This has led the Communist Parties to oppose, ignore or minimise the role of rank and file democracy and self-management. The Parties typically have too high an opinion of their own role and tend to lack confidence in the autonomous initiatives of mass organisations that do not have a party content.

Clearly there are dangers as well as creative possibilities in the dialectic between parties and masses, representative and rank-and-file democracy. If the tension degenerated into a destructive conflict it could open the way for counter-revolutionaries to step in. The formulas brandished by some groups on the far left like "dual power" or the "outflanking" of the traditional "reformist" organisations once these have come to power, far from offering a panacea could scarcely lead to any thing other than defeat. But if the general staff of the Left, having arrived in power with a controlling position in the organs of representative democracy, proved incapable of opening up a positive dialectic with the mass organisations and movements, with the agencies of democracy from below, then such a destructive conflict will be inevitable—whether or not there is an extremist group consciously calling for it. This is not principally a problem of organisational conjunction, but of political method. What is needed is a continuous and realistic monitoring of the balance of forces, not to give way before it, but in order to be able to modify it. There must be a combination of realism and decisiveness, of prudence and audacity; easy tactical solutions should be avoided like the plague, as should all opportunist gestures that would create false illusions in the masses. The leading bodies must constantly look to the base for collaboration and assistance, not for passive consent, but for a dialogue without which there can be no solution of common problems.

An equal responsibility rests with the base, especially with the activists and rank and file leaders (which are present in every section of society whether conscious or not). They must carefully take into account all the possible dangers of any situation, including the ever-present risk of counter-revolution; and they must judge to what extent the excuses of dangers and complexities in every problem which those above tend to allege, correspond with real objective facts.

In the course of our preceding exposition we have several times referred to aspects of the positions of the Eurocommunist Parties—either in their conception of Socialism or of themselves, or in certain aspects of their internal constitution and operation, that we consider to be at variance with their declared aim of a democratic road to socialism. Let us now draw these points together.

1. In general terms the model of socialism that these parties offer for their own countries is a democratic socialism which corresponds with their stated position that "socialism is a higher stage of freedom and democracy; it is democracy carried to its ultimate consequences". But they flatly contradict this principle by accepting the regimes of Eastern Europe as socialist. Naturally this raises a question as to how deeply the principle is held.

2. There is no basis to the claim of the Communist Parties to be the sole custodians of "the scientific Marxist method". This is an obstacle on the democratic road to socialism. When they announce (as in the PCE Manifesto and Programme) that "we are in a better position than any other working class party to lead the proletariat and its allies in the fight to win political power and achieve socialism"; when they continually proclaim "the correctness of their line"; when they describe the Communist Party as *the* party of the working class and go on from that to deduce that since the working class is to have a hegemonic role within the new social bloc then the Communist Party must necessarily play a leading role in a socialist society—then they make a serious error. No party, group or individual can reasonably claim exclusive possession of "the scientific method of Marxism": it is available to any party—although few in history have so far shown themselves particularly competent in its use. The Communist Parties have few reasons to congratulate themselves on their own performance. What kind of "scientific method" was it that allowed them to take the Stalinist system as their model of

socialism for several decades, deriving from it a totally false notion of the relationship between socialism and democracy which they are only now correcting, and which encouraged them to believe for decades that capitalism had reached the limit of its historical possibilities? Not to speak of the immense anthology of wrong analysis, false predictions and bad policy that one could compose from the history of the CPs (such as the PCE's regular prediction nearly every year of the imminent fall of Francoism). It is true that other parties have not been backward in such matters either—but at least they do not lay title to scientific precision.

Marxist science, like any other science, needs free discussion, full freedom to criticise, the frank admission of error; there can be no authorities for it that are immune from criticism. The very structure of the Communist Parties contradicts this need. It is not an accident that for a good many years most of the new developments in Marxist thought have originated outside the ranks of Communism, which have been noteworthy less for their contribution to "Marxist science" than for their crass theoretical indigence. As for the argument that the PCF regularly puts forward to justify its claim to be *the* party of the working class (the only one)—that it contains within its ranks a majority of politically active workers, this could just as well be used to define the German Social-Democrats or the British Labour Party as *the* parties of the working class in their countries.

The reason why this concept is not merely wrong but also an obstacle to the realisation of socialism, is that it relegates every other working-class organisation (other parties, unions, organisations etc) to a subordinate role—a position they are not inclined to accept. It therefore causes division and confrontation. It is also an obstacle to the development of proletarian self-organisation, which is a basic precondition for the working class to become the hegemonic class. There are further negative effects we could mention.

3. The absence of any adequate measure of internal democracy, which we have already noted above is also in direct contradiction with a democratic road to socialism. In spite of

some changes for the better since the epoch of Stalin, democratic centralism continues to be, essentially, centralism. How else can one explain the apparent ease with which the Communist Parties achieve near unanimity on the most difficult questions, accept sudden turnabouts in line, affirm the correctness of predictions and policies that events have shown to be in patent error? Then there is the fact that officials in these parties are virtually assured of a secure job for the rest of their lives, so long as they continue to support the authority and the opinions of the principal leader. "Elections" by party congress are always well prepared in advance by the same machinery that ensures the approval of the leadership's policies, so that the leadership becomes in effect cooptive and self-perpetuating. There is little opportunity for the membership and the masses to participate in public discussion of problems in the party press or other media. It is difficult for organs of grassroots democracy to make their views known to the party. All of these failings at the level of internal democracy can be summed up in the famous ban on internal tendencies.

Taken together these points give rise to a serious question. If the hopes of the Communist Parties are realised and they become the main leading force under socialism, but are themselves not democratic in their own mode of operation, how can it be a democratic form of socialism? If these Communist Parties also accept the possibility (in the Eastern countries) of an undemocratic form of "socialism", is it not more likely, if they remain unchanged, that such would be the kind of socialism that would result from Communist hegemony? To questions of this kind the Communist Parties reply that the party is one thing and society is another. How can there be any basis for such fears, they say, when the party accepts pluralism, promises to respect the decisions of universal suffrage, defends all civil liberties and stands for the separation of the party from the State? To which we reply that a form of words or even a legal framework may be one thing and the reality quite another. Formally and juridically the regimes of Eastern Europe enjoy a soviet or a popular democracy, with pluralism, liberties, separation of party from State. But behind the legal façade the Party provides the real machinery of power; and the party is anti-democratic to its very core. Let us imagine for a moment that the Communist Parties which hold absolute power in those countries began to function democratically. The result would immediately be the start of a process of democratisation such as occurred in Czechoslovakia. When a party plays such a dominant role in a society it is obvious that there will be a close relationship between the nature of the party and the nature of the society. If the Communist Parties do not change their present style of "democratic centralism" there are two possible results. Either they will be condemned to a subsidiary role in the realisation of democratic socialism, because as the workers grow in consciousness and take a more active part in politics, they more and more reject that kind of party. Or if, taking advantage of circumstances and of the immaturity of the masses, the Communist Parties should come to exercise the function of leadership, there will be a serious danger of an evolution into an authoritarian kind of State.

There is a third alternative—which is the most desirable from the point of view of the general interests of socialism and the working class. That would be for the Eurocommunist parties to continue in the direction of their present evolution until they have transformed themselves into genuinely democratic parties. Although there have been some hopeful signs (more in some of these parties than in others) the decisive measures have still not been taken. In its Manifesto and Programme, for instance, the PCE announces that "as soon as the basic freedoms have been won we will open a great debate within our ranks on how a proletarian party of the new type should function under conditions of democratic legality. On the basis of the widest possible prior debate, delegates will be democratically elected to a congress which will have the task of deciding the form of organisation and the methods that best correspond to the kind of party we are building, a party which is called to act as the guarantor of the progress of the Spanish revolution towards a democratic form of socialism".

Only time will tell whether the deed will match the word or whether the existing party machinery will produce a fictional debate and fictitious elections. (Two observations I would make in passing—why is the PCE called on to be the *guarantor* of the progress of the Spanish revolution?—Can there be an undemocratic form of socialism?)

If, irrespective of the good intentions of those concerned, the democratic road is not to lead us to a new version of "undemocratic socialism" or to a new social-democratic version of modernised capitalism, then we will need Marxist parties of a new type. (I emphasise parties, not a single party.) Whether they call themselves Communist or Socialist, they will have to be genuinely democratic, maintaining the closest links with the working class and the whole of social reality (the two things go together). Their Marxism will have to be open to any useful contribution from the social sciences and from every current of advanced modern thought if it is to prove itself capable of developing the theory of revolution in the West. They will have to transcend the old Leninist notion—pseudo-scientific and authoritarian—of the party as director of the masses, which history has shown can very easily degenerate into manipulation of the masses. Instead of encouraging the cult of leaders these new parties will rather foment a critical spirit among the masses, increasing their capacity to intervene and exercise control within parties and trade unions, as within other mass organisations and organs of representative and grass-roots democracy.

For the countries of Southern Europe and for every advanced capitalist country, the democratic road is the only possible road to socialism, but it will not be an easy road to follow. The Communist Parties of France, Italy and Spain have a great deal to contribute to a successful completion of the journey, providing they can make the necessary changes in their own internal life as well as in their political positions; they must make room for democracy within themselves as well as in society.

Between the Two Superpowers

A hundred and twenty-seven years ago, in one of his genial flashes of intuition, Marx foresaw that Europe would lose its independence and world supremacy to what was then a rising young power—the United States of America—unless it could accomplish in time its "second great social revolution", the socialist revolution. At that time the threat from the colossus of Tsarist Russia which towered over the rest of Europe seemed more immediate. In spite of its feet of clay, it still had the armed might to act as gendarme against any European revolutionary movement, and in that capacity delivered the *coup de grâce* to the "spring of the peoples", in the revolutions of 1848.

Marx's premonitions have proved prophetic. Every attempt at revolution in Europe has been frustrated; while since Yalta and its division into zones of influence, it has virtually lost all independence. In the Western half of Europe the armoured columns, missiles and multi-national corporations of the US have been installed with no intention of withdrawing. The White House dictates what parties may or may not be represented in the governments of Europe, under what conditions and within what limits. In the other half of Europe the fragile empire of the Tsars has been replaced by the iron grip of a Eurasian superpower which, empty now of all the revolutionary content of the October Revolution, has transformed the states of Eastern Europe into a series of satellites as far as the frontiers of Russia.

Because of this historical context the dawn of a genuine form of socialism, of which we can now see a faint promise on the horizon, which would be the outcome of the long march of the European workers' movement and the advanced forms of Western thought, confronts a double threat. In the midst of the tissue of tensions, contradictions and common interests that are a feature of relations between Washington and Moscow, on one issue there is complete accord—both would find intolerable the existence in Western Europe of any *soci-*

alist (as opposed to social-democrat) democracy. Each in its own way, for its own reasons, vies with the other for the honour of attacking those elements of the European Left that are proposing a democratic socialist alternative to the capitalist crisis.

It is in this context that the Sonnenfeldt-Kissinger doctrine effectively proposed a kind of "imperial historic compromise" with Moscow.[64] (We have referred earlier to the speech which the then Secretary of State and his councillor for West European affairs made to the meeting of US ambassadors in Western Europe in December 1975). In effect the representatives of the capitalist superpower are saying to their "socialist" counterpart: Gentlemen, we accept that you have now attained the level of a world superpower. We cannot reverse that situation. Let us therefore reach some general understanding. We are ready to help you reach the level of consumer provision that your people desire. We have an interest in the stabilisation of your empire in Eastern Europe, because otherwise the aspiration of its peoples to freedom and independence might lead to a catastrophic clash which would not suit either you or us. We also acknowledge that if Communist Parties get into government in Western Europe it will not be your doing. (Kissinger was quite straightforward on this point: "It is not the Soviets who are responsible for the unstable situation that presently confronts us in West Europe. A Communist Western Europe would be a headache for them too. They would probably prefer not to see the Communist Parties come to power in West Europe".) Let us get this matter sorted out. We did not lift a finger when you so expeditiously wiped out the attempt at socialist democracy in Czechoslovakia. Now it is France and Italy which are likely to raise the same problem, and they are within our zone of influence.

Can we assume that this proposal for a "historic compromise" between the two superpowers has been withdrawn or substantially altered by Carter's arrival in the White House? The main thinkers of the new team—Carter himself, his Secretary of State Cyrus Vance, and the veteran Krem-

64. *Le Monde*, 14 April 1976.

linologist Zbigniew Brzezinski were all involved in the so-called Trilateral Commission which clearly spelled out a world strategy. (The Commission, which was set up in 1973, acquired its name from its guiding theme, which was the need for closer "association" between the three main centres of advanced capitalism—North America, Japan and Western Europe—in other words, a more complete integration of advanced capitalism under US hegemony).[65] Various analysts of the Trilateral strategy have made it clear that their differences with Kissinger's line are more questions of method and tactics than of strategy,[66] which suggests that there are not likely to be major differences as far as the Left in Western Europe and the socialist opposition in the Eastern countries are concerned. Brzezinski, for example, thinks that America could strengthen its negotiating position vis-à-vis Moscow if Soviet influence in the Eastern-bloc countries could be reduced. This is undoubtedly one of the intentions behind Carter's campaign for "the defence of human rights" in the Soviet bloc. To see in that campaign anything more than a tactical manoeuvre motivated by local aims of US policy in home or foreign affairs would be to close one's eyes to everything that US imperialism stands for. (For example there is the desire to refurbish the standard of US democracy, now so tarnished by the series of barbarities and scandals from Vietnam to Watergate.)

Whereas the response of Kissinger, Haig and other representatives of the Ford administration to the possibility of the Left taking power in some of the countries of Western Europe was to make direct threats, some of the statements made by "Trilaterals" and especially by Carter himself, indicate a change of tone—and have even been interpreted by some of the Communist leaders as proof of a change of

65. The "Trilaterals" are a group of economists, bankers, industrialists, politicians and intellectuals drawn from these three areas. The organisation is based in the USA and North Americans account for 74 out of their total number of 200. Leading figures include the present head of the French government, Raymond Barre; the head of FIAT, Giovanni Agnelli; and the president of the giant Japanese conglomerate Mitsubishi, Chujiro Furino.

66. See Diana Johnstone "Une Stategie 'Trilaterale' " in *Le Monde Diplomatique*, November 1976.

substance. But the official statement of the State Department on 6 April 1977 sets the record straight. First comes the liberal velvet glove: "We are convinced that the position of a Communist Party in any given country is a question that can only be decided by the people and the government concerned. We do not intend to interfere in the process by which that decision will be taken." Then comes the imperialist fist: "However this does not mean that we have an attitude of indifference. We attach a great importance to our ability to work together with the countries of Western Europe on matters of vital interest. Our ability to do so could be obstructed if these governments came to be dominated by political parties whose particular habits, ideas and practice are foreign to our basic democratic principles and to the common interests on which our relations with Western Europe are based."[67]

The State Department spokesman would not enlarge on what was meant by a government that was "dominated" by a Communist Party, as opposed to the warnings of Ford and Kissinger against governments with Communist "participation". At what point does tolerable "participation" become intolerable "domination"? One may conjecture that a Communist majority, even if that was a reflection of the popular vote, would prove intolerable, as would Communist control of certain key ministerial positions such as those of Defence, Foreign Affairs or the Interior. But perhaps the most widely applicable, most concrete interpretation we can put on it is that any government would be unacceptable to Washington (regardless of the measure of Communists included) which proposed a real socialist transformation.

George Ball, one of the most eminent "Trilaterals", explained in an interview with the *Washington Post* in May of 1976[68] that there was no shortage of measures that could be taken without any need to resort to the use of armed force. "Instead of making threats like Kissinger, it should be enough for us to give notice to the Italian people that the entry of Communists into their government might endanger their

67. *Le Monde*, 8 April 1977.
68. D. Johnstone, op. cit.

economic well-being. To produce the desired effect it would
be better if this warning were to come from Italy's European
neighbours rather than from the United States ... which
should be content for once to play a non-speaking part. The
EEC obviously has a whole range of measures available by
which it could seriously reduce the level of Italian economic
activity: imposing restrictions on agricultural imports, with-
holding regional assistance. As a final sanction the other
members could expel Italy from the Community."

The German Chancellor Helmut Schmidt was shortly to
reveal that Kissinger and Ford began to apply just such a
"coordinated strategy" soon afterwards, at the Puerto Rico
conference. Schmidt's revelations provoked an indignant
reaction from the French and Italian Left. "It is the height of
impudence", said Mitterand, "to assume that the peoples of
Europe will tolerate much longer the harness of a new Holy
Alliance".[69] But Carter gave his unconditional support to the
"Puerto Rico strategy" just prior to his election. Criticising
Ford and Kissinger for making their threats too blatantly, he
commended Helmut Schmidt for "showing the right attitude
when he says that it (the entry of Communists into the Italian
government) would jeopardise German aid for Italy. I think
when the democratic countries express themselves frankly,
energetically and openly they are simply exercising their
influence in a legitimate way."[70]

Is not the State Department statement of 6 April 1977
simply a ratification of this line? That is the only policy that
can be expected from American imperialism, if a Left government that is genuinely committed to carrying through a
process of democratic socialist transformation comes to
power in Rome, in Paris or in any other European capital.
Western Europe occupies a key position in the world-wide
web of US imperialism, in economic terms as well as for
reasons of military strategy. It is a major base for the multi-

69. *Le Monde*, 20 July 1976. Schmidt revealed on 16 July that at the Puerto Rico
conference the Western nations had decided that if the PCI entered the government
they would suspend economic aid to Italy.

70. D. Johnstone, op. cit.

nationals. In addition to that it possesses a special feature that we referred to earlier, and which is seldom remarked—the start of a socialist transformation in Europe would have immediate repercussions on the working class and progressive forces in America and could become an internal problem for the USA.

As for the other superpower, there are two reasons why Moscow looks warily or even hostilely at the prospect of a socialist transformation in Western Europe. The first, which we have already discussed, is the effect it would have on the internal order of the Soviet State and the entire Eastern bloc. A socialist order that included national independence, democratic liberties, a plurality of political parties and independent trade unions, would be a highly subversive example to the workers of the Soviet empire and to its oppressed nationalities, which would rouse them to struggle for their own freedom and a genuine socialism. We should not forget that it was to prevent the development of just such an alternative that Czechoslovakia was invaded in 1968. Moscow's other concern is that the onset of a process of socialist transition in Western Europe, by destroying the existing international *status quo*, would seriously upset the two superpowers' search for an "imperial historic compromise" which would secure the technological and economic cooperation that is every day more urgently needed by the Soviet bloc economy.

Whereas in general the forces of the European Left have little doubt about the nature and rationale of US imperialist policy, the same cannot be said in relation to the Kremlin, because of the illusions about the nature of the Eastern regimes and because of the esoteric language it uses. When Suslov or Ponomarev belabours the Western Communist Parties for their abandonment of the "dictatorship of the proletariat" and "proletarian internationalism", for "betraying the socialist revolution and capitulating to opportunism and bourgeois conciliationism" they are not speaking a revolutionary discourse. What they are really demanding is that these parties should return to the fold and once more accept

Moscow's lead; that they should reaffirm Brezhnev's neo-Stalinist dictatorship as the true form of socialism. If they were to accept such a *diktat* the Western parties would have to break all their ties with the people of their own countries, cast aside the banner of democracy, lose all chances of making alliances with the other socialist forces and definitively close the way to socialism for Western Europe.

The functionaries in the Kremlin do not delude themselves that they have much hope of reversing the present trend of development within the West European Communist Parties. What is feasible—and has already occurred in a number of countries—is the prospect in the medium or long term of splitting the parties, raising up against them "new" Communist Parties on the old model. When the Kremlin assaults the weaknesses (real and imagined) of the Eurocommunist parties and their opportunism, it chooses to attack "from the Left". If takes every possible advantage of the resonance that still exists within these parties of the old themes, the soviet mythology, the "revolutionary phrase". The purpose of this ideological artillery is to prepare the ground for breaking moral and political solidarity with the Western parties once the decisive test of power arrives. On the assumption that the experience of power will prove to be a failure, the Kremlin is poised to exploit the resultant situation to the full; it is then that it will provoke splits and do decisive battle with Eurocommunism. In a few countries where the opportunity has arisen such splits have already occurred—as in Greece, Austria, Spain and more recently in Sweden and Britain. In the French party, during the course of an extensive debate on the Soviet Union, a pro-Soviet current has apparently found its Joan of Arc in the person of Maurice Thorez' widow, Jeannette Thorez-Vermeersch. A former member of the Central Committee and Political Bureau, she resigned those positions in protest over the attitude the leadership of the French party took to the invasion of Czechoslovakia. After a long silence she has now returned to the fray in the pages of *Le Monde*, to make a sharp attack on the positions that Elleinstein has advanced on the Soviet Union, and through him on the party itself. It was noted within the French party that the reappearance of Thorez' widow coincided with the stepping up of direct and indirect criticism of the PCF from Eastern Europe. Only a few days before the appearance of her article one of the main leaders of the Czech party had been describing the policy of the French and other Eurocommunist parties in terms that almost amounted to a charge of class treason. Some active party members consider that there is a real possibility of a split by some of the unconditional supporters of the Soviet Union.

Caught as they are between two fires, the forces that are struggling for socialism in Western Europe must be able to protect themselves from the attentions of both superpowers. A strategy for socialism in any of these countries will have to cover the problem of securing the defence and national independence of each country and of Western Europe as a whole, firstly against the Atlantic superpower and secondly against the Eurasian superpower. It is clear too that the cause of West European independence is closely connected to the question of national independence for the countries of the Soviet bloc and for the right of self-determination for the nationalities within the Russian state. Although the question is naturally not posed in the same way as in the Third World, the need to maintain national independence against both imperialisms is a very real one for the countries of Europe, which is indissolubly linked to the question of socialism.

The Eurocommunist Parties find themselves in this difficult and dangerous international setting without any common international policy. It seems indeed that they are deliberately putting aside the problem, preferring instead to limit themselves to the adoption of purely *ad hoc* defensive positions. One after the other they have proceeded to follow the example of the PCI in accepting the framework of the Atlantic Alliance, that functions to insulate them from the unwelcome attentions of the other superpower, which are likely to become more pressing should the CFs come to power. But if they do not also work out a policy aimed at progressively reducing US influence in Europe, based on

a realistic assessment of the changing balance of forces—
the degree of consciousness and level of mobilisation of the
popular forces within each country, the kind of solidarity
they can expect from abroad, including support from anti-
imperialist states in the Third World etc, and the effects
of superpower rivalry—they will find themselves in an impasse.

A similar problem is posed in relations to the other superpower. For here too Eurocommunist policy is purely defensive. Even if we accept that in this matter as in all else it is
necessary to tread cautiously, it is difficult to understand why
the Eurocommunist parties have not developed a more active
form of solidarity with the growing forces that are striving for
a democratic socialist renewal within the countries of the
Soviet bloc. The only reason we can see for the timorousness,
the total inadequacy of their response so far to appeals for
their support from oppositional forces in Eastern Europe is
what we have referred to as "umbilical cord of ideology"
which still connects the Eurocommunists to the Eastern
regimes. Yet it is clear that if there is not at least some
improvement in the degree of independence and democracy
enjoyed in those countries the cause of socialist revolution in
the West will be impeded and imperilled, just as in Russia
after 1917 the frustration of the revolution in the West
resulted in the isolation and involution of the socialist revolution in the East.

The third necessary dimension to the international
policy-making of the Eurocommunist parties is the process of
European unification. There is a real need for the Eurocommunist Parties and every other genuinely socialist force in
Europe to make an active intervention in this process in the
interests of the workers and peoples of Europe. For it is a
general principle that the building of socialism cannot be
completed within the confines of a single country, much less
of a small country like those of Western Europe. National
frontiers have become an impediment to the proper planning
and development of productive forces which are already
organised on an international scale. The only way in which the

countries of Europe will be able to regain and secure their independence vis-à-vis the superpowers, and ensure that their fragmentation is not an obstacle to socialism, is by increasing voluntary cooperation. As soon as there are moves towards increased independence and democracy in the Eastern part of Europe, so should the idea of a united working-class Europe be extended to encompass them too. For any perspective of this kind, it is obvious that the socialist forces should participate in the present European institutions. But that participation should be on the basis of a united policy of struggle against the multinationals, against monopoly capitalism and all reactionary forces. If such a policy is to obtain results it cannot be confined to existing institutions, it must also develop into joint mass actions by the various national detachments of the working classes, with close coordination between their various political and trade union organisations. So far we have seen only the germ of this kind of cooperation. It is true the divergences between the PCF and the Italian and Spanish parties now seem to have been reduced to the question of the PCF's attitude to elections to the European parliament. But no start has been made towards the development of a common policy with the Socialist parties and those elements of Social-Democracy that are in favour of a genuine struggle to build a socialist Europe.

Finally there is the problem of the Third World. It would be absolutely essential for a socialist Europe to conclude alliances with those peoples and States that have been brought into conflict with imperialism on their road to development—they are just as much in need of solidarity from the workers of Europe as the latter are in need of their support. This is another field in which so far only some bilateral initiatives and the CERES proposal for a "geographic compromise" have shown much progress. Yet in this field too the objective pressures of the present world conjuncture demand a joint approach by the Eurocommunist and Socialist parties of Europe and by the anti-imperialist forces of the Third World.

* * *

Eurocommunism still hesitates to accept itself as such, it doubts its own capabilities, simultaneously affirms and denies its identity. In internal political questions and in international problems, the three main parties of Eurocommunism have up till now avoided thorough discussions or common positions. One of the reasons—not only tactical, but oedipal—has been fear of worsening relations with Moscow. This was noticeable at the Madrid summit. But another quite different reason for their resistance to joint action is that none is absolutely secure in the direction of its own policy. All three parties oscillate between the temptation of social-democracy—which would reduce the democratic road to socialism to the level of social-democratic reformism—and a genuine desire to create the conditions for a socialist alternative to the capitalist crisis. They all announce measures of internal democratisation, but cannot persuade themselves to consign to the archives their anti-democratic centralism. All three claim they have superseded their Stalinist pasts, yet they continue to shrink from any complete reestablishment of historical truth.

Eurocommunism contains the possibility and the hope of overcoming—within advanced capitalism—the general crisis of the communist movement. But it could just as well turn out to be its swan song. This uncertainty should be a cause of concern not only to Communists, but to all forces with a socialist perspective—because it is just as difficult to envisage a transition to socialism in the West which does not include the Communists as one which excludes the Socialists. If socialism does not throw over the practices of social-democratic reformism, or if Eurocommunism fails to live up to its promises, then there may occur a restabilisation of capitalism for a whole historical period, blocking the road to socialism in Europe for the indefinite future. The road we have to travel is a narrow and difficult one and many dangers lie in wait for anyone who departs from it—to deny that would be to breed illusions. But it is a possible path which we must attempt. For it remains as true today as ever that the only alternative to socialism is barbarism.

Madrid, April 1977

4.

Further Steps Towards
a "Western Schism"

The requisitory unleashed by Moscow against Eurocommunism in the June edition of the magazine *New Times* has since confirmed many of the theses advanced in this essay. Some readers had considered my assertion that "In Eurocommunism we can discern the beginnings of a 'Western Schism' within the international communist movement . . ." to be far-fetched. But the publication of Santiago Carrillo's book *Eurocommunism and the State* and the Soviet leadership's virulent response give eloquent testimony that this is indeed the direction that events are taking.

We indicated in Chapter 2 that the obvious deterioration of relations between the CPSU and the three major parties of Eurocommunism in matters of politics and ideology had reached a critical point in the course of 1976. The conflict had grown steadily more bitter ever since the first general public confrontation between the Eurocommunists and the Soviet bloc at the Berlin Conference in June 1976. In spite of the prudence of the French and Italian positions at the "Eurocommunist summit" in Madrid in March 1977, the Eastern bloc leaders who were meeting at the same time in Soia took alarm. It seems likely that it was at this meeting that they planned the present offensive. The publication shortly afterwards of Carrillo's book simply provided the detonator.

There seem to be two reasons why the explosion came at this time. One relates to the content of the book. In it Carrillo went further than he had ever gone before in his comments on the nature of the Soviet system, which is the most contentious of the issues that separate the Eurocommunist positions from those of Moscow. Carrillo no longer tried to get around the problem with references to a "primitive socialism". However ambiguous and hesitant his formulation, he clearly raised doubts about the validity of the regime's claim to be socialist. Having once broken the "umbilical cord of ideology" of subservience to Moscow, Carrillo was left free to explore all the profound contradictions of Soviet foreign policy. His findings on that score proved no more acceptable to the Soviet leadership than his views on the nature of their domestic system. Moscow could not remain silent any longer.

The second reason why the Kremlin chose the general secretary of the Spanish party as its target was that he was more vulnerable than either of his colleagues in the PCI or PCF. Neither the political base nor the national role of the Spanish party came close to that of the parties of Marchais or Berlinguer. A target was needed and Carrillo appeared to have cast himself in the role. But although the article in *New Times* sought to distinguish between "good" and "bad" Eurocommunists, it was in reality directed against the movement as a whole. Moscow is well aware that far from representing some pathological deviation from the general strain of Eurocommunism, Carrillo's position is simply the logical conclusion of its general line of development. We have demonstrated how, given the well established fact that any kind of democracy is conspicuously absent from the regimes of Eastern Europe, the guiding principle of Eurocommunism, the belief that socialism is impossible without democracy, implicitly denies their socialist character. No amount of skill in "dialectical" juggling—at which the PCI is particularly adept—will be able to prevent the other Eurocommunist parties from sooner or later following in Carrillo's footsteps.

To those who "clamour for the PCI to deny that the USSR is socialist", *Rinascita* replies: "No, and again no . . . This is still a question of politics; of judging what is the real role of the socialist countries in the world, what they are, what they represent in the real balance of world forces in these years."[71]

71. *Rinascita*, 1 July 1977.

So it is not a question of theory or of ideology, but of politics. Irrespective of the true nature of the East European states, the reality is that they think of themselves as "socialist countries", and they do have a certain (massive) weight in the world balance of forces. Don't let us upset the tiger by telling him he is not what he says he is—because of one thing we may be sure, he isn't made of paper!

We do not think we err in assuming that Berlinguer and Marchais share to a greater or lesser extent the opinions that Carrillo has expressed on the real nature of the Eastern countries. But they do not operate within the same political constraints—and that is the basis on which they will decide when they are free to say what they think. Carrillo needed some spectacular way of asserting his independence from Moscow and his democratic *bona fides*. In spite of the merits of the PCE in the clandestine struggle against Franco's dictatorship, in spite of the party's criticisms of certain aspects of the East European regimes, wide sections of the Spanish population—including many workers—found the image of the PCE still too closely associated with that of the Soviet bloc dictatorships. This was undoubtedly one of the reasons for the party's poor showing in the Spanish elections of June 1977. Obviously it was not easy under conditions of clandestinity to make the party's political positions widely known, but if it had ever released a statement as clear then as Carrillo had made now it would have certainly broken the barriers of silence. It would also have had a very positive effect on the development of the theoretical positions and internal life of the party and lent credibility to its declarations of democratic intent.

Santiago Carrillo has complained that if only the Soviet attack in *New Times* had come a few weeks before the elections "it would have been worth several hundred thousand extra votes for us".[72] What then if it had come twenty years before, on the occasion of the 20th Congress of the CPSU? Or even ten years before, when the USSR invaded Czechoslovakia? Even if it is true that the PCE was ahead of the

72. Press Conference of 27 June 1977 in Madrid. See *Mundo Obrero*, 29 June 1977.

majority of Communist Parties in its attitude to the Czech affair, it had been as backward as the rest so far as the question of the Soviet Union was concerned. Yet this was an especially serious issue for the Spanish Party, because for 40 years the struggle against a fascist dictatorship had given the theme of democracy paramount importance in Spain. When it finally took the step that was needed, it was not even in time to win those extra votes with which Carrillo was so concerned. Indeed it is only because the PCE's relative weakness in the Spanish political process relieves him of the responsibilities of a Marchais or a Berlinguer that Carrillo could take the step he did. He had nothing to lose and a world of credibility to gain.

Because of the much stronger social and political base possessed by the French and Italian parties and the fact that they are drawing daily closer to a governmental role, Marchais and Berlinguer are both obliged and inclined to give more importance to demands of diplomacy. The maintenance of good relations with Moscow is now starting to be a matter of State interest for the two parties, for a whole new series of considerations (the need for a countervailing force to set against the other superpower, the need to make sure that their privileged relationship with the Kremlin is not usurped by the Socialists or some other force). Nor is this simply a question of opportunism, although opportunism there is in large measure. The problem they confront—of trying to adopt a clear Marxist position on the Eastern countries (which would imply among other things clear expression of solidarity with those progressive forces that are seeking to transform them), without provoking a complete rupture with Moscow—is a tremendously difficult yet decisive one. It is made yet more difficult by the attitude of the Soviet Union, which insists on a clear choice—either you accept us as a socialist, indeed a "developed socialist state" or we won't play any more.

A certain divergence between Carrillo on the one hand and Marchais and Berlinguer on the other was already discernible at the Madrid "summit", where the French and Italian parties turned down the Spanish suggestion of a denunciation of attacks on human rights in the Eastern countries. The Kremlin's strategists sought to exploit differences of this sort to the full in their attack of 23 June. This can be seen both in the article itself and in the way the dispute has developed since then.

The article sought to make a clear distinction between two different "interpretations" of Eurocommunism. One was "the interpretation of the forces on the Left, including the Communist Parties".[73] Although the *New Times* article expressed a number of reservations about the term itself, it acknowledged a valid aspect of this interpretation: it was after all undoubtedly a fact that "there is a common basis to the strategic theses of several of the West European parties, and more generally of parties in those capitalist countries with a high level of economic development". *New Times* was quick to point out that there is nothing novel about this: did not Lenin indicate the necessity of taking into account each country's national peculiarities? The article then proceeded to enumerate various reasons why, in spite of this degree of validity, the notion of "Eurocommunism" was mistaken. One objection was that which was first raised by the leaders of the Italian and Spanish parties themselves—the fact that non-European parties share similar positions. But the basic objection was that behind these convergences of strategy Eurocommunism appeared to allude to some "unidentified specific form of communism", when it is well-known that "communism—if we are talking about real, scientific communism—is one and one only: the foundations of which were laid down by Marx, Engels and Lenin, whose principles are followed by the contemporary communist movement." However, there is at least room for argument over this "interpretation".

Not so with the other, "more far-reaching interpretation of Eurocommunism: the construction which the representatives of the bourgeois world chose to put on it from the very first". Santiago Carrillo's version belongs to this second category, to

73. See the text of the French edition of the Soviet journal: *Temps Nouveaux*, 26, 1977.

which *New Times* ascribed the following intentions: "Its first aim is to set the Communist Parties of the capitalist countries of Europe against the Communist Parties of the socialist countries. Its second is to denigrate the reality of socialism in those countries that have already created a new society, especially the Soviet Union. Its third is to reject all the joint conclusions of the European Communists, the goals they have set themselves of struggle for the interests of the working class and all toilers, in the cause of peace, democracy and social progress. To this (Carrillo) opposes a completely different programme, which amounts to maintaining the division of Europe into two military blocs and, even worse, the reinforcement of the aggressive Nato bloc." In a footnote the authors add that "It would be superfluous to quote concrete proof that such a position in no way corresponds to the interests of peace or socialism". Indeed—just as it would be superfluous to demonstrate that there is not one iota of truth in these accusations.

For fifty years since the installation of the Stalinist dictatorship, from the Moscow trials to the present indictment of Carrillo, the Kremlin has used the same charges until they now form a stereotyped bureaucratic ritual. Then as each new "turn" in the political line has so demanded, the charges have been cynically belied, so that now nobody seriously pretends that they have any relationship at all to the truth. Nevertheless as a political act, an index of the Kremlin's thinking and intentions, they must be taken seriously. It is in this light that we shall examine some of the more extreme charges brought against Carrillo in the *New Times* article.

To justify the last point quoted above, its authors blatantly distorted Carrillo's position on the process of West European unification—which is in fact the official position of the PCE and very close to that of the Italian party. In his book Carrillo had declared that "our aim is a Europe independent of both the USA and the USSR, a peoples' Europe directed toward socialism in which our own country will be able to preserve its own personality." This was twisted by *New Times* into the following: "the author's main theme is the 'union' of Western

Europe on an anti-Soviet platform", linked to "the idea of a scission into two separate parts of the continental forces of democracy and the communist movement", the Western section of which would be destined to follow "a 'third' or 'intermediate' road that lies in some suspiciously indeterminate territory between capitalism and socialism". The article concluded that "Santiago Carrillo's interpretation of Eurocommunism serves only the interests of imperialism, the forces of reaction and aggression."[74]

To tell the truth, apart from the opinion we quoted above, Carrillo hardly touches on the subject of European unity in his book, nor on the PCE's policies on the subject. It will still be some time before the question of Spain's entry into the EEC is resolved, and it will also be some time before the PCE enters government (unless in a very minor way). For the time being its role in this respect is insignificant. Both the PCF and the PCI on the other hand are close to the exercise of governmental responsibility; the PCI is already to some extent exercising it. So Moscow has a real immediate interest in their "European" policy. Even if they do not reach governmental office, both parties have a major impact on political developments in their respective countries. The large amount of space devoted to this subject in the *New Times* attack on Carrillo only makes sense therefore if it is interpreted as being directed at the PCI, the party which has gone the furthest in this matter. It is significant that, whereas on all the other issues raised in the polemic against Carrillo the leadership of the PCI has taken an ambiguous attitude, they immediately assumed that the reference to European unity was meant for themselves, and restated their position.

Reading between the lines of the attack on Carrillo we can register a growing fear on the part of the Soviet Union at the prospect of a united Europe independent of both superpowers. At the root of this fear is not so much any belief that such a united Europe would be capable of matching the might of the enormous military machine that lies beyond the Elbe, but rather the realisation that it is impossible to envisage such

74. Santiago Carrillo, *Eurocomunismo y Estado*, Barcelona 1977, p. 134.

a Europe coming into being unless the popular working-class forces have won hegemony, unless it is socialist.

It is not that the Kremlin is worried that such a united Europe would be limited to the Western half of the continent—quite the contrary. It is afraid of the increasingly strong pull such a democratic socialist Europe would exercise on the Eastern half, tending inexorably towards the dissolution of the military blocs and the unification of the two Europes on the basis of democratic socialism. What it really fears is not a Europe under American domination—which is the Europe of Giscard, of Schmidt, of Andreotti that we have already—but a peoples' Europe independent of both superpowers.

In his replies to the Soviet attack Carrillo has suggested (as he had in his book, though less explicitly) that for Moscow "the existence of a Europe of NATO under US control provides the justification for the existence on the other side of another Europe under Soviet control".[75] To which we might add that without that "control" the "real socialism" that prevails throughout the Soviet *glacis* might very rapidly dissolve into a series of "Czech springs". Moscow is also afraid that the persistent and virulent conflict with Maoism in the East will now be combined with contestation from Eurocommunism in the West, and that the respective "European" strategies of the Chinese and the Eurocommunist Parties will converge. It is not without a certain malice that the PCI press has noted the beginnings of what appears to be a change in the attitude of the Chinese Party towards the Italian Party. The North Koreans too expressed sympathy for Eurocommunism on the occasion of Tito's recent visit.

But for all the importance that Moscow undoubtedly attaches to the "European question" it does not constitute the main axis of the Soviet attack on the general secretary of the PCE. That is reserved for the "Soviet question", the definition of the socio-political system that has been raised on the ruins of the old Tsarist empire. It is obvious that this question is not only important at the level of theory, it has

75. Press Conference of 27 June.

had, and will continue to have, an enormous importance at the level of practical politics. (In reality, of course, the two questions are closely connected, since if Eastern Europe were genuinely socialist its power of attraction over the West would have been such as to resolve all these "questions" long ago. But we know what the real course of history has been.) We have already dealt with two of the most important aspects of this problem as they touch our theme of Eurocommunism. We shall now add to these a further two, without pretending that we have thereby exhausted the problem.

We may first note that it is vital for the Soviet ruling class that its regime be acknowledged as socialist by the international workers' movement. Its claim to the title forms such an essential part of the official ideology of the Soviet state, of its ideological justification for its existence before the eyes of its own people, that it would be quite impossible for the leadership of the CPSU to renounce it. Contrary to what certain simplistic analyses might suggest, it is not just the repressive police action of the vast Party-State machine that maintains the greater part of the Soviet peoples and of Soviet communists in passive conformity. There is also a highly efficient mechanism of ideological alienation which makes truly virtuoso use of the mystified inheritance of Marx and Lenin.

For Social-Democratic parties to deny the socialist nature of the Soviet regime is for Moscow quite insignificant, since for decades it has been dinned into their peoples' heads by the official ideology that Social-Democrats are the agents of the bourgeoisie within the workers' movement. Moreover, there is no example of a successful Social-Democratic transition from capitalism to socialism. More or less the same holds for the criticisms of Left groups. But when some of the most important and prestigious of the Communist Parties—yesterday the Yugoslavs and the Chinese, today those of Western Europe—reach the same conclusion, it is a very serious matter. (We might note that there is no novelty in the ideas Carrillo puts forward in his book. Leading theorists and politicians from other parties and independent investigators have said as much before. What has caused such a big impact among the peoples and parties of Eastern Europe and the communist movement at large is the fact that it is here repeated by the General Secretary of the PCE.)

Moscow has only one solution for such a situation: to break with the parties concerned—as it did with Tito, with Mao, with Dubcek—announcing that, like the social-democrats, they have fallen into the hands of agents of the bourgeoisie and of imperialism. New parties, true to the ideas of "Marxism-Leninism" can then be created to stand against them. This reaction is not just a case—as some of the experts on these matters would have us believe—of the Soviet leadership slipping back into the pattern of its previous mistakes. For the new ruling class there is no room for compromise on this matter. On each occasion Moscow has applied a specific tactic. Sometimes the path may be long and tortuous, but in the end it reaches a point where those that have dared to question the socialist nature of the Soviet system must either capitulate or break with it. The day that there is a change in this order of things will probably signal the fact that the question is being asked from within the system too; as has already occurred in Hungary and Poland and Czechoslovakia.

In the case of Eurocommunism, the Soviet leadership has served notice in *New Times* that it will be a hard battle but that it is certain of victory: "We shall emerge victorious from the struggle against the bourgeois splitters and those who seek to introduce their ideas into the ranks of the communist movement. The European Communists have already come through more than one difficult test and will certainly prove capable of defeating this new attempt to divide their ranks." For the moment they have placed the "bourgeois splitters" in two categories. There are those like Carrillo who have already revealed their abominable intentions by throwing doubt on the socialist nature of the Soviet system and the altruistic character of its foreign policy; and there are those like Berlinguer and Marchais—and certain other leading figures in the PCE—who have yet to cross this fatal Rubicon.

But they all receive the same warning—however long the fight, there will be no quarter given. In the meantime the ground must be prepared by a combination of heavy ideological bombardments and a series of intrigues and manoeuvres designed to exploit any internal differences within each of the Eurocommunist parties and their differences with each other. This can be clearly seen from the way in which the conflict has evolved since it emerged into the open with the *New Times* article.

One important point which emerges is that Moscow has encountered on this occasion a much greater reluctance to support its operation within the Communist movement than was the case with Tito or Mao. Of all the Soviet-bloc parties, only the Czechs and the Bulgarians responded to the clarion call of the *New Times* article to take arms against Eurocommunism. They had been mobilised earlier anyway. The Poles, the Hungarians, even the East Germans showed a certain reluctance and had to be urged into the lists by the Soviets. It seems that the Cubans decided not to publish the first *New Times* article, limiting themselves to the later ones which were less aggressive. The Rumanians, well known for their oppositionist position within the bloc, came out in defence of Carrillo, who was received by Ceaucescu. As for those CPs that are in power but do not form part of the Soviet bloc, the Yugoslavs have clearly declared their support for the PCE general secretary, while simultaneously accusing the Soviet Party of a return to the "Stalinist methods" that it used against Tito in 1948. They released their statement on the eve of Tito's visit to Moscow. The Koreans too have come to Carrillo's defence. So far as we are aware the Chinese and Vietnamese have not declared their position.

Among the Western parties, Moscow has received—as was to be expected—the backing of the minuscule North American party, which always gives the Kremlin unconditional support, and of the small parties of Austria, Denmark and West Germany (which one communist journalist referred to some time ago as Moscow's "fifth column" within the West European CPs). The parties of Britain, Belgium, Sweden and

Norway and the Greek party of the Interior, plus of course the French and Italians, have all come to Carrillo's defence, some more energetically than others. (We do not have complete information, so this is not an exhaustive list.) We can therefore say, in brief, that there has been a much more marked reluctance than in similar cases in the past to support Moscow's operation. At the same time we should note that there have been various ambiguities and reservations within the defenders of the PCE too.

In the first place, the parties that spoke out for Carrillo did so independently of each other (while on the other side it is clear the offensive was planned and coordinated by the CPSU). In an interview which Carrillo gave to *Le Monde* a few days after the appearance of the *New Times* article he was asked whether the three principal parties of Eurocommunism were going to issue a joint statement. His reply was categorical: "No, we shall each be responsible for our own defence."[76]

In the second place, what they were defending against Moscow was essentially the right of each party to its independence, to decide for itself on questions of politics and ideology. In most cases they did not enter into the questions that Carrillo had dealt with in his book. We have already quoted one of the exceptions to this, which was the PCI's reaffirmation of its European policy. Another was an article by the General Secretary of the Swedish party in which he declared that Carrillo's main ideas were in line with the Swedish party's programme. Although some of the other parties agreed on the need for a "scientific debate", none of them actually initiated it. On the key question, his challenge on the socialist nature of the Soviet Union, Santiago Carrillo stands virtually alone—so far as stated positions are concerned—among the other Eurocommunist parties. The PCF, for example, made the most discreet intervention possible, publishing a news item on an inside page of *L'Humanité* which stated that: "The general secretary of a Communist Party has been directly attacked for having published a book,

76. Interview in *Le Monde*, 28 June 1977.

some chapters of which are open to criticism, but which do not warrant insult or anathema . . ." and went on to defend Carrillo's rights.[77]

The Italians and Rumanians in particular have made it clear that they do not agree with Carrillo, although both parties, more particularly the Italians, have acted as mediators between the PCE and the CPSU. In the course of an interview he gave to some American journalists, Ceaucescu defended Carrillo while at the same time making it clear that it was necessary "not to counterpose to the form of socialism that has been realised in some countries the form of socialism that the Western Communist Parties propose to realise."[78]

As for the PCI, the article we have already quoted from in *Rinascita* is sufficiently eloquent. Naturally Ceaucescu does not want the kind of socialism which has been realised under his control to be put on trial, and Berlinguer already speaks on these matters like a member of a future government that will wish to have good "state" relations with Moscow. Neither wants to grasp this nettle. Let matters of this sort be left to theoreticians who don't have political responsibilities! No doubt they say to themselves in private "why did Carrillo have to meddle in something that is not his own field?"

It is well known that at the time the Soviet offensive was launched a delegation from the PCI was on its way to Moscow. After no doubt many hours of difficult discussion with the representatives of the CPSU, a joint communiqué was issued. It spoke of "an atmosphere of sincerity", the euphemism used to indicate that neither side has shifted from its fixed positions. The whole Italian press shared the opinion of *Corriere della Sera* that in tone and content it was more like "a communiqué issued by a meeting of two great powers, than by two fraternal parties." Pajetta, who had headed the PCI delegation, announced that "they had surveyed with great frankness . . . all the current problems of the international workers' movement, especially those that are presently the

77. *L'Humanité*, 7 July 1977 (our emphasis).
78. See *Il Manifesto*, 20 July 1977.

object of controversy and polemic" (an obvious reference to the conflict with Carrillo). But this was not reflected in the communiqué. One can only deduce from the statements made by members of the Italian delegation on their return to Rome that while they gave Carrillo their political support, they dissociated themselves from his views on the USSR and Eastern Europe—and not only on the question of the nature of the system. When Pajetta commented that "Moscow is no Vatican", he was disputing Carrillo's reference to Moscow as the Holy Office of the Communist Church. Another member of the delegation, Macaluso, revealed that "the Soviets say they do not want the polemic with the PCE to get out of hand, still less to extend it to the other West European CPs. What they want is to get down to a calmer discussion which will not oblige anybody to renounce particular criticisms they may have of the USSR, but which cannot involve a total condemnation."[79] In other words, the Soviets offered to tone down their attacks on Eurocommunism, providing the latter did not adopt the extreme position of denying the socialist character of the Soviet regime. It seems the Italians have accepted the *quid pro quo* and have undertaken to convince the Spanish party. No doubt this was the mission of the delegation that was sent to Madrid shortly after (composed of second-rank figures) to have discussions with the PCE leadership. Although the attacks on Carrillo continued in subsequent *New Times* articles, they were more moderate in tone, reflecting the compromise that had been agreed with the PCI. But the attacks on Eurocommunism in general continued with varying degrees of virulence in the press of the Soviet Union and its satellites.

In selecting Carrillo as the priority target in their operation against the Eurocommunists, Moscow's tacticians took into account the existence of differences within the PCE and between the PCE and the PCF and PCI on a number of questions. They had prepared their "bomb-shell" well in advance, but they chose to detonate it on the occasion of the meeting of the PCE Central Committee convened to discuss

79. *L'Unità*, 5 July 1977.

the party's poor election results. They expected to get the support of the party president Dolores Ibarruri and possibly of one or more other members of the leadership. It may be that Dolores Ibarruri accepts that the Soviet Union is not the ideal model of socialism, let alone the correct model to apply to Spain; but she was obviously not going to accept that anyone should question its socialist nature. The way the discussion went in the Central Committee showed that Moscow had not miscalculated, even if its highest hopes were not fulfilled.

The statement which was approved by the Central Committee in reply to the *New Times* article limited itself to a reaffirmation of the independence of the Spanish party, of its "Eurocommunist road" as the "only valid alternative for the advance to socialism", but all it had to say on the taboo subject was that the methods which Moscow had employed in this case "are one of the reasons why we find it impossible to present the so-called *true socialism* of the Soviet Union and similar countries as the ideal model of our socialist society."[80] When one of the more recent members of the Executive Committee, who is known for his independent critical spirit, proposed that the text include a specific reference to the absence of democratic freedoms in the USSR, the idea was turned down to avoid a clash with Dolores Ibarruri.

The Central Committee also agreed to publish the complete *New Times* text with a detailed refutation, but three months later the decision has still to be carried out. Have the efforts at mediation by the Italian and Rumanian parties produced a change in the PCE's plans? At all events, Santiago Carrillo himself has continued in the weeks following the *New Times* charges to reaffirm his position vigorously. He has strongly condemned the Soviet methods, not restricting himself to the means of expression available to the Party, but making full use of the mass communications media both within Spain and internationally. At the time of writing he has announced that he has accepted a "private" invitation from

80. *Mundo Obrero*, 29 June 1977.

the University of Yale and is shortly going to visit the United States.

It is difficult at the moment—in mid-September 1977—to foresee how the conflict is likely to develop. In my opinion the most likely perspective is that it will become more bitter, not in a linear fashion, but with moments of comparative calm interspersed with periods of great tension. For the time being Moscow is trying to keep its criticisms of the Eurocommunists within tolerable limits and the French and Italian parties, which for the moment are inclined to accommodate to them, are being used to moderate the "Spanish fury". But any transition to a governmental role in Rome or Paris will give rise to a host of contradictory pressures on the Italians and the French. Some of these will impel them in the direction of maintaining good relations with Moscow, while others will rather impel them towards a more radical divorce from the "socialism" of the Eastern-bloc countries.

Moscow has more than one card to play. At the same time as it tries to reach a compromise on the terms we have indicated, it is also preparing the ground for a more drastic kind of "solution" should other Eurocommunist Parties follow Carrillo across the Rubicon. There are many pressures driving the Western Parties in that direction: the inner exigencies of the development of a democratic road to socialism; the fact that the debate about the nature of the Soviet system is no longer the property of a handful of ideologues, but has been opened to large sectors of the best educated cadres of the workers' movement. There is also the matter of the inability of the ruling classes of the Eastern countries to forgo repressive measures against their internal oppositionists (how are the Eurocommunist Parties going to react to such repression?). Then there are further pressures from their socialist allies and from the groups on the far left.

Aware that there is a real danger of the Eurocommunist Parties "crossing the Rubicon", Moscow is preparing to split them and create alternative parties "true to Marxism-Leninism". Obviously this would not be an easy task, but one should not underestimate the possibility. In the worst case

Moscow will not hesitate to create such a "Communist Party", however small, in opposition to any party that supports positions such as Carrillo has already espoused.

There is another possibility of which we should not lose sight. If the policies of Eurocommunism prove incapable, together with other forces on the Left, of making a reality of the democratic advance towards socialism, if they appear to the masses to be nothing but a variation of social-democratic management of the capitalist crisis, then it could well happen that whole sections of the party membership and the working class will turn their backs on the Eurocommunist leaderships. Some of these could well go to the extreme Left, which also casts doubts on the "socialist" nature of the Eastern countries; but another portion could be seduced by the Leftist language in which Moscow couches its attacks on the Eurocommunists. The strategists in the Kremlin are prepared for such a contingency, and are patiently and tenaciously working to create the conditions which would enable them to take advantage of it.

In France they are waiting for one of two eventualities—either that the Union of the Left will break up before the elections, which would result in the disintegration of the leading group around Marchais which is associated with the evolution towards Eurocommunism, or that the Union of the Left comes to power and then fails. In Italy they are waiting for the present policies of the PCI to fissure the relationship between the party and the masses, between the leadership and the base. In Spain their expectation must be that the present orientation of the PCE towards a "historic compromise" with the Centre party—the party of the King and of Suarez—will destroy the credibility of the leading group around Carrillo in the eyes of important nuclei of the party and the working class.

Meanwhile Carrillo has gone even further in calling for a "government of national concentration" which would extend from the Francoist Right (Fraga's party) to the PCE. That policy is intended as an imitation of the strategy of the PCI, but at least in Italy the Party not only has a powerful position in parliament but also in the whole fabric of State and society; while Christian Democracy has a large left-wing which has a genuinely democratic base among popular masses and the workers. None of this applies in the Spanish case. As the June elections showed, the PCE is as yet a weak force. If we discount Catalunya it scarcely exceeded 6% of the vote. Although it probably still has the largest trade union organisation, the socialist and other trade unions are growing fast. While the only point in common between Italian Christian Democracy and the Spanish CDU (Centre Democratic Union) in that they are both the chosen political instruments of their respective big bourgeoisies. But the CDU did not arise out of resistance to Franco—it is rather Francoism converted in its last quarter of an hour; nor does it possess any social base, let alone a popular left-wing like the Italian DC. On top of all this the relationship between Socialist and Communist Parties, at least at the parliamentary level, is precisely the reverse of that in Italy. The Left won the 15 June elections in every decisive region of Spain, and the dynamic since then has tended to tip the balance steadily in its favour. There is therefore the possibility in the medium term, if not sooner, of a Left government. But if there is to be a real alternative power, more will be needed than simply a parliamentary victory; there will have to be a united coordinated political and social bloc with a concrete programme for the transformation of Spanish society. Unless there is some unforeseeable change in the political map of Spain, the only force which can reasonably exercise hegemony within this bloc is the Spanish Socialist Workers Party (PSOE). But it will need a policy of alliances with the PCE and other forces on the Left which has not up till now figured in the PSOE's strategic thinking.

For its part the PCE has apparently turned all its attention towards securing a "historic compromise" with the Right, and rather than work towards Left unity it is seeking to push the PSOE in the same direction. Santiago Carrillo has won himself a great deal of credibility in a short time by this policy, with the Spanish Right. It would not be surprising if this—as much as his resistance to Moscow—lay behind the invitation of the secretary general of the PCE to America.

Among Carter and the Trilaterals the idea has been gaining ground that the Eurocommunist card could be played towards two ends: to weaken the Soviet bloc by stimulating the internal opposition in the Eastern countries and (at least in Southern Europe) to help European capitalism out of its present difficulty. Moscow's policy, on the other hand, is more and more directed towards the conversion of Western Europe into a series of Finlands and its efforts to reach a compromise with the Eurocommunist Parties should be seen in that light. In this sense the negotiations between the CPSU and the PCI may have a much wider significance than the Carrillo affair.

Carter's policy is to destabilise the continental equilibrium—not with any intention of provoking a major showdown with the other superpower, but rather to ensure a more favourable apportionment in the "imperial compromise" which both sides desire; Moscow seeks instead to freeze the equilibrium of the *status quo*. Yalta revised or Yalta frozen. *Vót Voprós!*[81] as Brezhnev would say, making it clear that the first alternative leads to nuclear war, the second to a guarantee of peace.

The Eurocommunist prospect of a united Europe independent of both the Soviet Union and the United States may seem, in the light of these two alternatives, a fine mirage. But if the Left were able to win power in France, in Italy and in Spain and could tap popular energies for a real advance towards socialism, always by the method of deepening, extending and strengthening democracy, then much might change. There are many reasons to be pessimistic. But was it not always so on the eve of some great historical upheaval?

September 1977

81. That is the question!

Index of Names